PATHWAYS TO ULSTER'S PAST
Sources and resources for
local studies

Peter Collins

The Institute of Irish Studies
The Queen's University of Belfast

Published 1998
The Institute of Irish Studies
The Queen's University of Belfast

This book has received support from the Cultural Diversity Programme of the
Community Relations Council which aims to encourage acceptance and
understanding of cultural diversity. The views expressed do not necessarily
reflect those of the NI Community Relations Council.

British Library Cataloguing-In-Publication Data.
A catalogue record for this book is available from the British Library.

ISBN 0 85389 693 3

Set in Ehrhardt
Printed by W. & G. Baird Ltd, Antrim

Front cover: Detail from Etching in Layers series by Anne M. Anderson

CONTENTS

LIST OF ILLUSTRATIONS

The illustrations are reproduced by kind permission of the following people and institutions: pp 11, 45, the National Gallery of Ireland; p 13, The Queen's University of Belfast; pp 24, 29, 57, 135, the Trustees of the Linen Hall Library; p 47, the Council of the Royal Irish Academy; p 62, the Trustees of the National Museums and Galleries of Northern Ireland; pp 88, 96, the Deputy Keeper of the Records, the Public Record Office of Northern Ireland; p 99, the Environment and Heritage Service (DOENI); p 114, the Trustees of the Fermanagh County Museum; p 118, the Trustees of the Cavan County Museum; p 139, the National Library of Ireland.

PREFACE

The purpose of this book is not to explain how to go about the practice of local history. Rather it aims to show where local historians, teachers and students should go to obtain the raw material for their work. How this material is then processed is a different matter altogether and outside of the scope of this volume. The geographical area is the historic nine-county province of Ulster. The period covered begins with the early 17th century, coincidental with the Plantation of Ulster, and ends with the years around Partition. Chapter 1 briefly defines the nature of local history and looks at locales and units of administration in Ireland. There follows a discussion on the changing nature of the records, due to the exigencies of the times in which they were being made. Chapters 2, 3, 4 and 5 examine the records or sources from the 17th to the 20th centuries.

In Chapter 6 records are then examined in a generic sense; religious, business, educational, photographic, etc. Archives and record offices are covered in Chapter 7; museums in Chapter 8; and finally libraries are looked at in Chapter 9. These last three are considered under the categories of accessibility to the public and their main holdings and collections.

I have been very reliant on the information kindly furnished by the professional staff of all the record repositories. This has included guides and lists usually written by staff. In these instances, I have replicated this information, within the overall format of this book. What is listed is that which I believe to be the most helpful and I make no claim that it is exhaustive.

ACKNOWLEDGEMENTS

First, I wish to acknowledge the Cultural Traditions Group, now called the Cultural Diversity Programme, of the Community Relations Council, which awarded the Jack Magee Fellowship in Local History. This book is the result of the research undertaken for the fellowship.

I am grateful to Professor Brian Walker, Director of the Institute of Irish Studies, for the help and facilities provided by the institute during my fellowship there. I also wish to thank him for his very helpful advice at the manuscript stage.

I am much indebted to Dr WH Crawford, formerly of the Federation of Ulster Local Studies, for his advice and constructive criticism throughout the project. I am grateful to Tony Canavan, also formerly of FULS, for his advice and help. Janet Lundy of FULS was also of great help with resources. Dr William McAfee of the University of Ulster at Coleraine; Dr William Nolan of UCD; Professor Kevin Whelan, now Director of the Keogh Study Centre, University of Notre Dame, Dublin; and Fr Peter McGuinness, Inniskeen, Co Monaghan were generous with their advice and information.

I was fortunate to be based at the Institute of Irish Studies among extremely knowledgeable colleagues and friends who were unstinting in their encouragement and advice, notably Angélique Day, Patrick McWilliams, Dr Art Hughes, Kate Newmann, Jane Leonard, Dr Caroline Windrum, Dr Gordon Gillespie, Belinda Jupp, John Fairleigh and Catherine Boone. I am further indebted to Patrick McWilliams for producing the index. On the publishing side, I have been very well served by the editorial knowledge, skills, experience and patience of Margaret McNulty and Catherine McColgan, who have greatly contributed to bringing the project to completion.

The staff of PRONI were very forthcoming with help and advice, in particular Trevor Parkhill (formerly at PRONI), Dr Roger Strong and Dr David Lammey. I received first-rate assistance from library staff who provided advice and access to their valuable Irish and local studies collections, as well as supplying copies of in-house guides to collections, etc. In this I am especially grateful to the following: Deirdre Armstrong, SEELB; Linda Greenwood, BELB; Lynn Buick, NEELB; Joseph Canning, SELB; D Reid and Margaret Kane, Fermanagh Divisional Library, WELB; Patrick Brogan, Omagh Divisional Library, WELB; Maura Craig, Central Library, Derry City, WELB; John Killen, Linen Hall Library; Roger Dixon and Sally Skilling, Ulster Folk and Transport Museum library; staff at the Ulster-American Folk Park library; WRH Carson, Armagh Public Library; Maura Pringle, QUB School of Geosciences Map Library; Dr Eilis Ni Dhuibhne, Gerard Long and Grainne MacLochlainn, National Library of Ireland; staff at the National Archives, Dublin; Siobhán O'Rafferty, Royal Irish Academy; Valerie M Ingram, Office of Public Works library, Dublin; staff at the Representative Church Body library, Dublin; Tom Sullivan, Cavan County Library; Mary Monaghan, Donegal County Library; Joseph McElvaney, Monaghan County Library.

Museum staff who were of great help include: Dr Vivienne Pollock and Trevor Parkhill, Ulster Museum; Dr Greer Ramsey, Armagh County Museum; Helen Lanigan Wood and Bronagh Cleary, Enniskillen Castle; Brenda Collins, Irish Linen Centre/Lisburn Museum; Grainne Loughran and Jonathan Bell, Ulster Folk and Transport Museum; Linda McKenna, Down County Museum; Felicity Devlin, National Museum, Dublin; Dominic Egan, Karl Kinsella and Michelle Boyle, Cavan County Museum; Judith MacCarthy, Donegal County Museum; Pat Long, Monaghan County Museum.

1

LOCALES AND UNITS OF ADMINISTRATION

The study of local history is expanding rapidly and widespread enthusiasm for the subject has been accompanied by increased status, within the community and in the academic world. We have come a long way in the last 100 years when the following was written:

> . . . But local history is despised amongst us in Ireland. We are superior to all that; we have grown cosmopolitan; we read about and take an interest in every country from China to Peru; but who would be so mean as to take an interest in his own townland. And yet the story of some ivy-clad ruin which he sees everyday, or a piece of history or even a legend connected with a place he knows well, will have far more inspiration for an Irish child and will be a greater stimulus to his thoughts, than the Classics which tell of Thermopylae or Marathon or Troy, or the romantic narrative of how Horatius kept the bridge in the brave days of old.

Notes written c.1900, found in the the 1960s in Old Blackstaff (Tattyboy) School, Co Monaghan, author unknown.

WHEN IS HISTORY LOCAL?

Usually local history refers to a specifically defined, delineated and discrete area, with the emphasis on the community in that area. Any source or resource that tells us about a particular locality constitutes the raw material of local history. However, what is under consideration, need not necessarily have happened in the area. For example we may include the impact on the locality of events that have happened elsewhere. This can include national and international events such as legislative changes, wars or economic depression. Local people, who have moved away, may still have something to say on the locality as in the case of emigrant letters to home. Memoirs or

1

indeed the published observations of visitors or travellers, all can have something to contribute to the history of a locality. All such sources must be used critically. Why were they written, when, by whom and for what purpose?

In order to appreciate properly the relevance of the many records pertinent to local history, we must have a proper grasp of the divisions and sub-divisions which, for administrative reasons, have been made in this country. Also, we need to define at the outset, the locales to which people feel a sense of attachment and how this has come about. The locale is delineated by historic divisions and administrative areas.

THE TOWNLAND

The smallest, most ancient and widely used of these locales is the townland. The 1901 census showed 60,462 in the whole of Ireland. There are about 9,700 townlands in Ulster. Townlands took their name from prominent topographical features, social customs, history or indeed a local family name. They vary enormously in size, due to the fact that they have been shaped largely by topography and land use. The average size is around 250–350 acres. Townland names are mainly of Gaelic derivation. Many have names derived from topographical features, for example ard (height), mor (big), beg (small), cul (corner) gort (field), moin (bog), annagh (marsh), derry (oak grove), carraig (rock), drum (ridge), slieve (mountain), tully or knock (hill). Others refer to man's intervention, eg bally or baile (settlement), of which there were 6,400, many now disappeared, kill (derived either from coill – wood, or cill – cell or church), dun, cathair, lios or rath (fort).

Most townland names are Gaelic, with only a small number coming from Norse, Norman or English. The Gaelic townland names presented little problem to many of the incoming Scots in the 17th century, particularly the highlanders, being so similar to the Scots Gaelic place-names that they had left. Some townlands do not appear on the *Books of Survey* of the 1660s. Others have disappeared over time, as evidenced on maps and surveys for different periods. The Ordnance Survey (OS) also created new townlands, some of which can be identified by the use of suffixes such as upper, lower, north, south, east and west. There is evidence that some of these predate the OS by a century. Many of the Gaelic townland names have been anglicised, a process which was given official status in the OS (see pp 42–6). The OS 6 inch maps are the most important official record of townlands.

As administrative units, townlands became important from the 17th century. They were used then as the smallest division for official surveys and for the granting and letting of land. The townland names were the official nomenclature in legal documents. Townlands were the smallest division in the Tithe Applotment Books and in the later Census and Valuation Books. It is to the townland that most country people refer, when identifying their place of origin, and to which they owe their fiercest loyalty. This attachment is one shared by all traditions in Ulster. Even in the cities of Belfast and Derry, townland names have survived to the extent that they are the usual neighbourhood identification as in Ballymurphy or Ballygomartin, or Shantallow and Altnagelvin. The easiest way to find townlands or any other unit in the Public Record Office of Northern Ireland (PRONI) is to consult the *Alphabetical Index to the Townlands and Towns, Parishes and Baronies of Ireland*, compiled during the censuses. This may be found on the search room shelves. Then go to the Computerised Geographical Index in the reception area, which lists the relevant records available.

THE PARISH

In Ireland we have the civil/Church of Ireland and Roman Catholic parishes, the former comprising anything between 5 and 30 townlands. The civil parishes are so-called because they were also used for non-ecclesiastical purposes as units of administration. Parishes in the formal sense in Ireland, date from the 11th and 12th centuries when the country was moving more into line with church organisation in the rest of Europe. This meant shifting the ecclesiastical centre of gravity away from the monastery to the parish and diocese. Until the end of the 11th century, the abbots of the great monasteries were more important than the bishops in Ireland. The Synod of Rathbreasail in the year 1111, which divided the country into 26 dioceses, each ruled by a bishop, changed all this and with it regularised the parochial structure of the country. This situation remained until the Reformation, the only change until then being the changing of church dedications from native Celtic saints to those of the universal church, by the Normans. The medieval parishes and dioceses and their buildings passed to the reformed church in the 16th century. At the same time, the dissolution of the monasteries resulted in church land and surviving religious houses largely passing into other hands.

The now Protestant churches and parishes in many parts of the country were largely bereft of parishioners, reflecting the insecurity and failure of plantation and settlement. The wars of the 17th century compounded this situation. However, the old medieval parish retained its importance as a unit of administration, now known as the civil parish. These were used extensively, as territorial divisions, in the land surveys of the 17th century. Since then they have consistently been a major administrative and surveying subdivision. According to the official alphabetical index there are some 2,445 civil parishes, large and small. There are 22 dioceses and four archdioceses in the Church of Ireland. The dioceses united to form the four provinces of Armagh, Dublin, Cashel and Tuam, each headed by an archbishop. There are no longer Church of Ireland archbishops of Tuam or Cashel. The dioceses of the Established or State church had a civil function, most notably in the probate of wills. This was within their jurisdiction until 1858 when the government set up a principal registry and 11 district registries to take over this function.

Roman Catholic parishes, during the Penal era, had of necessity to distance themselves from the medieval structure. The legal and economic strictures on clergy and flock meant that the ecclesiastical network survived only in a skeletal form. However, the mid 19th century witnessed a growth in parishes and dioceses, around magnificent new churches and cathedrals, reflecting not only the rise of Roman Catholic Ireland's ecclesiastical strength but also its burgeoning political power. The new Roman Catholic parish was more likely to reflect the actuality of where people lived, particularly in the emerging towns and cities, and it became a focus of much of the life of the community, for example as the spatial base of sporting organisations such as the Gaelic Athletic Association (GAA).

THE BARONY

The larger barony, of which there are around 300 in the whole of Ireland, is essentially an English unit of administration. Perhaps it was imported to replace the Gaelic *tuath* (tribal kingdom) of which only 97 are mentioned in the 11th century *Book of Rights*. The barony came into its own only in the 15th century. By the 16th century it was on the map in the literal and figurative senses, being included in all the state surveys and maps of land along with the county and townland. The barony was the second subdivision of the county and its continuing use in land transactions conferred on it both legal status and permanence. The usual number of baronies in a county ranges between seven and ten. In rare instances, a barony can straddle two counties. Then it is referred to as a half-barony in each. It was later used as a convenient subdivision for the enactment of the Grand Jury presentment sessions of the 18th and early 19th centuries. However, as a locale with which people identify, the barony is much less popular in comparison to other divisions such as the townland, parish or county.

THE COUNTY

As an administrative unit, this was a medieval English import, the first 12 Irish counties being set up in the reign of King John in 1210. However, Ulster, being beyond the Pale, remained largely untouched with only Antrim and Down having become counties (shired) by 1300. The rest of Ulster was shired by Sir John Perrott by 1584. The counties of Coleraine, Tyrone, Fermanagh, Cavan, Monaghan, Armagh and Donegal usually replaced the Gaelic lordships, O'Cahan, O'Neill, Maguire, O'Reilly, McMahon, O'Hanlon and O'Donnell respectively. The original county of Coleraine became Londonderry after the grant to the London companies. During the 17th century, the county became a major standard unit in the great schemes of land redistribution such as the Down Survey, the Civil Survey and the Books of Survey and Distribution. In the 18th and early 19th centuries, control by the nobility and gentry was maintained locally in the Grand Jury system. This had responsibility for local government functions, based on the county, and it was largely composed of landlords and their agents. The surveys of the Royal Dublin Society (see pp 27–8) at the end of the 18th and the beginning of the 19th century, were done on a county basis. The proliferation of county maps, at the end of the 18th century, largely sponsored by the Grand Juries, also helped reinforce county identity as indeed did the use of counties as units by the United Irishmen, the Militia and Yeomanry.

The county subsequently declined in importance in the 19th century. Under the Whig governments in the 1830s, certain functions, usually vested in Grand Juries, were lost to the counties. The most fundamental change was the establishment of the Poor Law System with separate administrative functions (see pp 5–6; 36–9). The spread of newspapers, in the latter part of the 19th century, was largely based on identification of each paper with a specific county. The GAA's adoption of the county, as a basis for top level competition, led to the upsurge of county loyalty bordering in some cases on fanaticism. Politically the county was the basis for parliamentary constituencies in the country. The Irish Local Government Act 1898, empowering county councils, underlined the paramountcy of the county in local government administration. From the point of view of archives, the county is a very rational unit of organisation, centred on the county museum and library. There have been many single-author histories of counties, such as the landowner EP Shirley's *The History of the County of Monaghan*, 1877, 'dedicated to the noble and gentlemen' of Monaghan. In the present day, the popularity of the edited county histories of nobles published by Geography Publications reflect the continuing depth of interest in the county.

THE POOR LAW UNION

The Poor Law Union was introduced under the Poor Law Relief Act of 1838, as a response to the severe poverty, resulting from the long agricultural depression that followed the Napoleonic Wars. The country was divided into

130 (later 159) districts called unions in which local people were responsible for the care of the paupers in the area. This differed from the system in England where the parish was used as the division. However in Ireland neither the parish nor barony was adequate. This necessitated the introduction of another tier of local government and taxation, administered by elected Poor Law Guardians. The unions were made up of townlands, within an average radius of ten miles, centred on a large market town, in which the dreaded 'workhouse' was situated. The records of the Boards of Guardians can be found in the county libraries and PRONI and the National Archives (see chapters 7 and 9).

THE DISPENSARY DISTRICT

This was a sub-division of the Poor Law Union, set up under the provisions of the Medical Charities Act of 1851. There were 829 of these in the whole of Ireland, on average six to seven for each Union. A medical officer had responsibility for public health in each district. These districts were also used as divisions for registering births and deaths, under the 1863 act for the Registration of Births, Marriages and Deaths. This established a superintendent registrar's district based on the union and a registrar's district based on the dispensary district. In most cases the medical officer for the dispensary district now acted as the registrar for the same area. The returns for these registration districts, as they were now known, were indexed and housed at the General Register Office in Dublin, with master indexes for the entire country. It now houses these records for the whole country up to 1921 and for the 26 counties after then. The Northern Ireland registers and indexes are held in the office of the Registrar-General for Northern Ireland.

THE PROVINCE

The four modern provinces are based on the four ancient kingdoms of Uladh (Ulster), Laighean (Leinster), Connacht and Mumha (Munster) and a fifth, Meath, which was later merged in Leinster. The suffix 'ster' was a Norse adaptation. The kingdoms of Oriel and Aileach merged with Ulster in the 17th century. Ireland was first divided into four provinces, at the Synod of Kells in 1152, when the four archdioceses of Armagh, Cashel, Dublin and Tuam were formed. The Tudors attempted a form of government headed by provincial presidents, emulating the system in Wales and the north of England. However this took hold only in Munster, for a short period, and had faded out by the late 16th century. The province, in the past, has had acceptance as a cartographical and census division. Generally, Ulster unionists, for political reasons, identify with six counties, while nationalists adhere to the historic nine-county province, which is also the territorial basis of sports like GAA, rugby and boxing.

THE RECORDS

The changing nature of records results from the exigencies of each successive era. In this respect, the nature of the records themselves is as indicative of their period as the information they contain. Thus, the Gaelic period is recorded in the Annals of Ulster and Ireland and the Four Masters and in ecclesiastical and Papal records such as episcopal visitations and First Fruits (an assessment of clerical holdings for papal taxation). The English interventions in Ireland, from the Normans to the early modern period, are the subject of Calendars of State Papers, such as those of Elizabeth I and James I. In this era we are also served by reports of official travelling commissions such as the 17th-century Inquisitions of Ulster.

The 17th-century records are largely about confiscations and re-allocation of land resulting from the wars of conquest and the ensuing plantations. Sir William Petty played a major role in surveying and recording the hand-over of land and power from 'native to newcomer'. The 18th century, being a more settled period, is largely recorded in documents pertaining to estates and inheritance. The family and estate papers of the great Anglo-Irish families are reflective of both resident landlords and absentees and show the extent of the political patronage of the Irish nobility and their relationship to the local community. The work of the Ascendancy intelligentsia and gentry, in the arts and agriculture and the sciences, is a matter of record particularly in the proceedings and surveys of the Royal Dublin Society and the Royal Irish Academy.

Entering the 19th century, we become aware of the increasingly complex nature of state and society and the ever growing canon of official documentation, necessitated by the introduction of large-scale reforms in local government, poor law and land reform. The very professionalism of this new dispensation and its officials produced records of unprecedented thoroughness and accessibility, in an age of increasing accountability. In records such as the Ordnance Survey, the Poor Law Valuation and the Census, and the Parliamentary Papers, comprising official surveys and reports into every facet of life, we have a cornucopia of data of inestimable value to the local historian. Indeed Ireland, due to its special circumstances, was a veritable laboratory for the official record-maker and keeper. The changing nature of land-holding for example, gave rise to a mass of official reports and legislation. At the same time, the move away from tenancy to small-holdings and the residual home farm and demesne is the stuff of 19th-century estate papers, especially correspondence between landlord and agent.

The sources and resources that have consequently come down to us are stored in a variety of institutions, north and south. Because both parts of the island shared a common administration until 1921, there is great commonality of records. To an extent though, there is a problem for the Ulster local historian, in that some relevant records may be in the Republic while others are in the six counties of Northern Ireland. Also many records have disappeared through misfortune, and the insensitivity or folly of man. Most calamitously, as result of the fires, in the Surveyor General's office in 1711, and in the attack on the Four Courts at the start of the Civil War in 1922, many valuable records were lost. However the skill, dedication and ingenuity of archivists and historians, such as Tenison Groves, has been invaluable in mitigating these losses from alternative sources.

2

SIXTEENTH AND SEVENTEENTH-CENTURY RECORDS

TUDOR AND STUART STATE PAPERS

The Irish Record Commission 1810–30, prepared copies of calendars in one volume covering the reigns of Edward I to Henry VII. They went missing after the Record Commission was disbanded. Calendars for the reigns of Edward VI to Elizabeth I were recovered, but those of Henry VIII are still missing. The Irish Manuscripts Commission, set up under the Irish Free State, partly revived the work of the earlier Irish Records Commission. It was responsible for publishing, in Dublin in 1966, T*he Calendar of Irish Patent Rolls of James I*, a facsimile of the Irish Records Commission Calendar prepared prior to 1830. Much of the 17th-century material has to do with the dispossession of the Gaelic and Old English Roman Catholic families, in the Ulster Plantation and in the wake of the defeat of the Confederation of Kilkenny forces, which brought settler control of the land in the form of estates. Those who had fought in, and the adventurers who had financed the Cromwellian wars in Ireland, were largely paid with confiscated land and to this purpose, the government needed to have an accurate picture of land-holding.

PLANTATION RECORDS OF THE LONDON COMPANIES

The Public Record Office of Northern Ireland (PRONI) holds the records of many of the London companies which were given land in the Ulster Plantation. These have been catalogued and published and guides are currently being made available, the most recent pertaining to the Salters Company. These records are a rich source for the Plantation in Co Derry.

UNDERTAKERS 1612–13

As the basis of the Ulster Plantation, Protestant English and Scots landlords were granted land. The proviso was that they undertook to bring in Protestant English and Scots tenants and provide security for their holdings against native Irish attack, hence the name undertaker. Lists of undertakers in counties Cavan, Donegal Fermanagh and Tyrone are given in *The Historical Manuscripts Commission Report 4* (Hastings MSS, 1947) which is available in the major archives and libraries. See also Pynarr's survey in G Hill, *Historical Account of the Plantation of Ulster* (Belfast, 1877).

MILITIA, YEOMANRY LISTS AND MUSTER ROLLS

The 17th century in Ireland was one of frequent warfare. In Ulster the principal landlords had to draw up lists of the names of Protestant tenants they could assemble in an emergency. These had to be inspected by the Muster Master General, who recorded the names, ages and the types of arms borne. They are arranged by county and district within the county. All Protestant males, between the ages of 16 and 60, were liable for militia service. Surviving copies of militia records list the undertakers and sometimes the lists of tenants by parish or barony. The Muster Rolls for 1630, are in PRONI, ref. MIC/15A/52 and 53. Muster Rolls for 1630 for Donegal and Cavan are in the National Library NL Pos. 206. The county and area board libraries have some copies of these for their areas.

The PRONI leaflet *Your Family Tree 12*, gives details of generally useful Militia, Yeomanry Lists and Muster Rolls from the 1630s up to the 1830s. These are for all the counties of Northern Ireland and give references for local units, where appropriate. There are also muster rolls of regular army units raised in Ireland, PRONI ref. T/808/15196.

Table 1: Extract from a muster roll c.1630

The names of the Men and armes of the Town of Strabane.

1. James Gib provost	sword only
2. Hugh Knyland	sword and snaphance
3. Robert Comyn	
4. Henry Wood	snaphance only
5. Walter Wright	sword only
6. James Reynold	sword only
7. William Conyngham	
8. George Paterson	snaphance only
9. John Wallis elder	sword only
10. Neal M'Ilwayne	sword and snaphance

Table 1 is an extract from a muster roll c.1630 (showing the first 10 out of a total 208 entries), PRONI ref. T/808/15164.

THE CIVIL SURVEY OF IRELAND

This was carried out by Sir William Petty (1623–87), between 1654 and 1667. Petty came to Ireland in 1652, as physician-general of the army, to put its medical services on an efficient footing. He was an enthusiast for the Protestant cause. He supported the Restoration and was knighted in 1662.

Sir William Petty (1623–87), cartographer, doctor and political economist. (National Gallery of Ireland)

He wrote *Hiberniae Delineatio (The Anatomy of Ireland)*, (reprinted, Irish Universities Press, Dublin, 1970) a description of the land, people, politics and resources of the country. He was founder and first president of the Dublin Philosophical Society, in 1683.

The Civil Survey was done in the wake of the Cromwellian confiscations, as part of the imposition of central control. It gives a list of the principal landlords of each townland before and after the Cromwellian confiscations. This was to ensure that land ownership was solely in the hands of loyal elements and was used for taxation purposes. The barony was the basic territorial division. The survey was called 'civil' because it was connected to the civil authorities. It used the inquisition method through juries, made up of local worthies, who had intimate knowledge of their area. The Civil Survey was connected to the Courts of Survey which evaluated land-holdings. It contains a great deal of topographical description, information on boundaries, quality of land, area under timber, and important settlement features, arranged by county, barony, parish and townland. Unfortunately, in 1711 a fire in the Surveyor General's Office destroyed all the records kept there. In 1817, however, 84 copies of the survey were found in the library of Viscount Headfort at Kells, Co Meath. The Four Courts Fire in 1922 destroyed the official set, but some copies were found in the Quit Rent Office (the records of this are now held in the National Archives, as the Headfort Papers). What survives includes counties Tyrone (four volumes) and Derry (four volumes), held in PRONI, ref. T/371 and Donegal, five volumes of which are in the National Archives. Derry, Donegal and Tyrone; Kildare and Limerick have been reprinted by the Irish Manuscripts Commission and are readily available.

The format of the survey, shown in Table 2, gives an indication of the detail it yields to the historian.

Table 2: Headings used in the Civil Survey of Ireland (1654–67)

Proprietors' names in 1640	Denomination of lands	Number of plantation acres by estimate	Lands unprofitable and the quantity	Value of ye whole & each of the said lands £.s.d.

THE DOWN SURVEY

This was a mapped record, carried out by Sir William Petty, of the entire country. His contract, with the government, effective from 11 December 1654, was to 'admeasure all the forfeited lands according to their natural,

Detail from the Co Tyrone sheet of Sir William Petty's Hiberniae Delineatio, (The anatomy of Ireland) *first published in 1685. (The Map Library, The Queen's University of Belfast)*

artificial and civil bounds and to state whether the land is distinguished into wood, bog, mountain, arable, meadow and pasture'. It was not uniform, as Protestant lands were not measured or subdivided. It got the name from the method of drawing or setting down of all lands in Ireland confiscated in the Cromwellian era. It can be used in conjunction with the Civil Survey. The work was to be carried out 'within one year and one month, provided the weather was agreeable and the Tories quiet'. This Petty accomplished in record time. The survey was done by trained surveyors, who were either ex-soldiers or Trinity College students, who measured and plotted the confiscated land. They were instructed 'to protract your work upon single sheets of large paper by a scale of forty perches to the inch'. They travelled throughout the country, in all weathers, staying in poor lodgings and in permanent danger from the violent attacks that often befell travellers in those days.

The divisions used were barony, parish and townland. The forfeited land was identified by townland and shown on parish and barony maps. There was a general description of the soil, its suitability or otherwise. It also noted the rivers in the barony. The survey's 'Index of Observations' for each barony catalogues and describes the built environment such as castles, churches, houses and mills. Barony maps were a synopsis of the parish 'Plotts and Bookes of Reference'. Settlement items such as castles and churches are shown in rough sketches. Rivers, roads and hill land are depicted. Other information, on the more detailed parish maps, concerns landownership and land quality. The subsequent fate of these records was melancholy. The originals were partly destroyed in the fire of 1711 and the rest in the Four Courts in 1922. Remaining copies of parish maps are contained in the Reeves Collection in the National Library, as are a series of barony maps known as *Hibernia Regnum* and the Quit Rent Office maps and tracings. Copies are in PRONI ref. CL 11 7, and many libraries have copies of Down Survey maps.

BOOKS OF SURVEY AND DISTRIBUTION

Compiled, around 1680, these were, like Petty's earlier surveys, concerned with the redistribution of land after the wars of the mid 17th century and generally follow the same format. They were used to impose the acreable rent called the Quit Rent which was payable yearly on lands granted under the terms of the Acts of Settlement and Explanation. They were laid out on a barony and parish basis. They constitute a record of land-holding, before the Cromwellian and Williamite confiscations and also a list of people to whom the land was distributed. Thus it is possible to determine the amount of lands lost by the 1641 owners and to discover the names of the new proprietors.

Although the fire in 1711, in the Surveyor and Auditor Generals' Office, destroyed the official copies, an official called Taylor compiled substitute copies. These manuscript copies bound in volumes refer to counties Armagh, Down and Antrim, Fermanagh, Monaghan and Cavan and Derry, Donegal and Tyrone. There are copies in the National Archives, and the Royal Irish Academy in Dublin. In PRONI, they form part of the Annesley Papers refs. D/1854 and T/371. They consist of 22 volumes, each containing an 'alphabet' which is an index of denominations. There is a topographical description of each barony. The details include 'Proprietors in 1641 by the Civil Survey', 'Denominations of land by the Downe Survey', 'Number of acres distributed', 'Number of acres distributed', 'persons to whom distributed', 'Rent per annum payable to His Majesty'. An abstract of the Down Survey and the Book of Survey for County Monaghan is included in Shirley's *History of the County of Monaghan*, 1879.

THE CENSUS OF IRELAND 1659

This was compiled by Sir William Petty and estimates the overall population in round figures at 900,000. It contains the names only of those with title to land (tituladoes) and the total number of English and Irish residents in each townland. In Ulster, all counties, with the exception of Cavan and Tyrone, are covered. The manuscript was found last century in the papers of the Lord Lansdowne, copies of which are now in the Royal Irish Academy. It was edited by Seamus Pender and published, by the Irish Manuscripts Commission, in 1939. Hence it is known as 'Pender's Census'. This edition has in the introduction a discussion on the origin and purpose of the census. The Pender edition, including Donegal and Monaghan is in the National Library NLI 31041 ch 4. This is also being reprinted by the Irish Manuscripts Commission. Pender, on page xiii, gives the following summary tables showing the 1659 census returns classification of the population under the heads of English (E), Scottish (S), and Irish (Ir). Unfortunately English and Scottish were not separately enumerated. Pender cites Eoin MacNeill on the unreliability of figures which show that only in one barony in Co Antrim, namely Glenarm, were there any Scots and none at all in Co Monaghan. Also the proportion of seven English to nine Irish in Antrim is suspect. Indeed, the fact that there is no separate classification for Welsh is a drawback, given the large numbers who settled in Ireland in Tudor and Cromwellian times. In his history of Co Monaghan, EP Shirley quotes the entire reference in the census to the county.

The format of the 1659 census is parishes, townlands, numbers of people, tituladoes' names, English/Scots, Irish. Counties were subdivided into baronies and the information summarised on a barony basis. Barony lists of

Table 3: **Extract from the Census of Ireland 1659**

Province of Ulster

	County	Barony	Races	Total
Antrim	Antrim	620 E	841 Ir	1,461
	Glenarm	721 ES	743 Ir	1,464
	Massarene	1,007 ES	1,358 Ir	2,365
	Toome	730 E	778 Ir	1,508
	Belfast	2,027 E	1,825 Ir	3,852
	Dunluce, Cary and Kilconway	1,138 E	2,940 Ir	4,078
	Carrickfergus Town	831 E	480 Ir	1,311
Armagh	Armagh	450 ES	891 Ir	1,341
	Tiranny	108 ES	546 Ir	654
	Orior	193 ES	694 Ir	887
	Fewes Lower and Upper	373 ES	858 Ir	1,231
	Oneilland	1,269 ES	1,366 Ir	2,635
Donegal	Tirhugh	244 ES	1,474 Ir	1,718
	Boylagh and Banagh	285 ES	1,556 Ir	1,841
	Raphoe	1,825 ES	1,330 Ir	3,155
	Kilmacrenan	605 ES	1,550 Ir	2,156
	Inishowen	453 ES	2,678 Ir	3,131
Down	Lecale	1,071 ES	1,631 Ir	2,702
	Upper Iveagh	448 ES	2,149 Ir	2,597
	Lower Iveagh	1,352 ES	1,381 Ir	2,733
	Newry	166 ES	785 Ir	951
	Kinelarty and Dufferin	693 ES	763 Ir	1,456
	Castlereagh	1,363 ES	950 Ir	2,313
	Ards	1,447 ES	984 Ir	2,431
Fermanagh	(baronies are not given)	1,800 ES	5,302 Ir	7,102
Londonderry City		572 ES	480 Ir	1,052
	Tirkeeran	640 ES	979 Ir	619
	Keenaght	1,012 ES	1,215 Ir	2,227
	Loughinsholin	655 ES	1,431 Ir	2,086
	Coleraine (Town and Barony)	1,549 ES	1,201 Ir	2,750
Monaghan	(baronies are not given)	434 ES	3,649 Ir	4,083

names and numbers of Irish were appended. This Census is in PRONI with references to the following counties:

Armagh 1659 census MIC/15A/72.
Antrim 1659 census MIC/15A/72.
Fermanagh 1659 census T/808/15064.
Derry 1659 census MIC/15A/82.

CESS TAX

Cess was an abbreviation of assessment and was a form of tax imposed locally, especially in the 17th and 18th centuries, for various purposes. Often it was raised for the military provisions in an area as a replacement for the unpopular earlier practice of billeting. Cess tax accounts took the form of lists of names with amounts due. Cess was often a cause of rural disturbance. In most Ulster counties, cess-induced disturbances, among farmers and weavers, lasted from 1763 until finally quelled by the army, in 1772. The term cess was later applied to local or county rates as levied by parish bodies or by the Grand Juries. From 1765–1845 more than three-quarters of county cess was spent on road and bridge building.

SUBSIDY ROLLS 1662–6

Subsidy was a form of tax levied on all those whose goods amounted to over £3 value or who had land of over £1 annual valuation. The rolls list the nobility, clergy and laity who paid such a grant in aid to the king. They give their name and parish and sometimes how much they paid and their status or occupation. Subsidy rolls relate principally to the province of Ulster. Subsidy rolls for Ulster counties are held in PRONI as follows:

Antrim 1666	Subsidy Roll T/808/14889.
Down 1666	Subsidy Roll T/307.
Fermanagh 1662	Subsidy Roll T/808/15068.
Tyrone 1664	Subsidy Roll T/283/D/1.

POLL TAX RETURNS

These list the people who paid a tax levied on everyone over 12 years of age. They also give more detailed information, than is usual for the time, about these taxpayers. The records in PRONI are as follows arranged by county:

Armagh 1660	Poll Tax Returns MIC/15A/76.
Down 1660	Poll Tax Returns MIC/15A/76.
Fermanagh 1660	Poll Tax Returns MIC/15A/80.
Tyrone 1698	Poll Tax Returns MIC/15A/81.
Derry 1669	Poll Tax Returns MIC/15A/82.

HEARTH MONEY ROLLS

They listed the name of the householder and the number of hearths or fireplaces on which he was taxed at the rate of two shillings each. This was the result of the Hearth Money Act of 1662 and subsequent related legislation. The 1662 measure prescribed that

> every dwelling and other house and edifice . . . within this kingdom of Ireland
> . . . are charged with the annual payment to the king's majesty . . . for every fire
> hearth, and other place used for firing and stoves within every such house and
> edifice . . . the sum of two shillings . . . to be paid yearly . . . at the feast of the
> annunciation of the Blessed Virgin . . . and the feast of St Michael the Archangel,
> by even and equal portions.

Also known as 'smoke silver', it was collected by the sheriff of each county and his men. The area covered was called a 'walk', which was based on the nearest town but covered a much bigger area than the town. The names were arranged alphabetically by county, parish and townland. Tax was paid by every tenant rather than by the landlord. The poor, such as widows and the permanently unemployed, were included, in the early rolls, but were later exempted. The first roll accordingly indicated social and economic standing. In PRONI, hearth money rolls extant are recorded, by county. The rolls lasted until after the Act of Union in 1800. The hearth money rolls are regarded as the most reliable pre-census means of calculating the population. This was done by taking the number of houses returned in a year and multiplying it by an estimated average occupancy per house. However, the collectors did not always enter the correct number of dwellings. For example, if they were corrupt, they covered their tracks by not counting all the houses they had collected from. Another limitation on the efficacy of the rolls is the fact that the next comparable population survey is too far away in years, namely the Religious Census of 1766. Unfortunately the original rolls were destroyed in the Four Courts in 1922, though there are copies for some areas as follows.

Antrim 1669	Hearth Money Roll	T/307.
Armagh 1664	Hearth Money Roll	T/604.
Fermanagh 1665–66	Hearth Money Roll	T/808/15066.
Derry 1663	Hearth Money Roll	T/307.
Tyrone 1664	Hearth Money Roll	T/283/D/2.
Tyrone 1666	Hearth Money Roll	T/307.

For Cavan, there are hearth money rolls in PRONI for the parishes of Killeshandra, Kildallan, Killrenagh, Templeport and Tomregan. Donegal hearth money rolls for 1665 are in the National Library, Dublin NL MS 9583, the Genealogical Office GO538 and PRONI T/307/D. For Monaghan, the hearth money roll for 1663–5 can be found in *A History of Monaghan for Two Hundred Years 1660–1860* (Dundalk, 1921) by DC Rushe. This was reprinted by Clogher Historical Society in 1996.

Table 4: Hearth Money Roll 1666, Co Tyrone, Omagh Barony West Longfield Parish (some of the manuscript names were indecipherable).

Area	Name of tenant
Kerlees	Torlogh o'Morisan
(Kirlish)	Ouen m'Cosker
Bonytaile	Hugh o'Maghy
(? Bomackatall)	Patrick o'Raverty, Thomas Bane
Killmore (Kilmore)	Torlogh m'Brian
Drumquine (Drumquin)	Thomas Bersall
Drumenyfarbir	Edmund m'Kinley
(Drumnaforbe)	Ouen o'Morish, Turlogh m'Nakilly
Loghlehard	Edmond o'Donally, Patrick o'Conally, Patrick o'Murry, Art o'Donally
Cailevanagh	Ouen m'Illrowan
(Coolavanagh)	Redmund m'Guire, Cormick Boy
Dowis (Dooish)	Shan o'Carra, Rory m'Quade, Torlogh m'Brian, William m'Morish
Laghfrassin	William Woods (Leqphressy)
Coraghmulkin	Patrick o'Raverty
(Curraghamulkin)	Murtagh o'Haghy
Cornavvary	Hugh m'Vaghy
(Cornavarrow)	Tool m'Vaghy, Patrick o'Rude, Philip m'Nabe, Ouen m'Vaghy
Sopgally	Edmund m'Laughlin
(Segully)	Edmind m'Laughlin
Dressoge	Rory o'Molaghan, Art o'Lunine
Culkiragh	Henry o'Boylan
(Coolkeeragh)	Phelomy o'Hugh
Leaght (Laght)	Rory m'Illcollum, Donaghy o'Lunine
Maghereny	John Lucas
(Maghereny)	John Woods
Longfield	James o'Morish, James o'Donell, Mulmurry o'Morish, Ouen o'Neill, Ouen m'Sorley

44 hearths £4.8s

CO ARMAGH ATTAINDER 1689

PRONI has the record of the names of Protestants, in Co Armagh, attained by James II, ref. T/808/14985. Under the Attainder Act of 1689, disloyalty or treason could mean being outlawed, the forfeiture of estates, loss of civil rights, or even sentence of death. A nationwide list of those attained was

drawn up by the so-called 'pretended parliament' of James II held in Dublin. Had it been enforced, it would have effectively reversed the earlier forfeitures and plantations. As it is simply a list of names, it has limited use. For other areas, similar lists may be held in local libraries or contained in local histories.

3

EIGHTEENTH-CENTURY RECORDS

THE RECORDS OF THE IRISH PARLIAMENT

These are a very useful source for the local historian, given their comprehensive nature and because of the interventionist tendencies of that parliament in the localities. During this century, which was comparatively settled, it is in the records of the schemes of economic improvement emanating from parliament, that we can see changes in the local areas. The published *Journals of the House of Commons of the Kingdom of Ireland 1613–1791* in 28 volumes, are available in the Public Record Office of Northern Ireland (PRONI) and the National Archives. The appendices in particular have a vast array of local information. Thus, we learn about the great navigation schemes that wrought such changes locally, built on the edict or with the help of parliament. The act of 1729, encouraging inland navigation, produced the Newry Navigation from Lough Neagh to Newry, the Lagan Navigation from Lough Neagh to Belfast and the Tyrone Navigation from the river Blackwater to Coalisland. In addition, public grant aid was given to the first Marquess of Abercorn for his navigation scheme from Strabane to the river Foyle. The proliferation of the building of military barracks, during this period, at parliament's behest, has left a legacy of information about localities. There is a vast record of the many other public work schemes undertaken throughout Ireland in this era.

VOTERS, POLL AND FREEHOLDERS RECORDS

These are lists of people entitled to vote or actually voting, arranged on a county basis. Poll books recorded the votes cast as the secret ballot was not introduced until 1872. The lists gave the names and the address of voters. They also record the address of the 'freehold' on which his entitlement to vote was based. Voters' lists and freeholders' registers do not record how votes were cast. The franchise was limited on religious as well as property grounds. From 1727 to 1793, only Protestants, with a freehold worth at least 40 shillings, had the franchise. From the following year until 1829, the year of Catholic Emancipation, Protestant and Catholic 40-shilling freeholders could vote. In that year, 40-shilling freeholders were thrown off the electoral list, considerably reducing its size. A list of generally useful poll books and freeholders registers, for the six counties of Northern Ireland, is given in PRONI leaflet *Your Family Tree 10, Voters, Poll and Freeholders Records*, as follows.

Co Antrim
D/1364/1	'Deputy Court Cheque Book' Poll Book 1776.

Co Armagh
T/808/14936	Poll Book 1753.
T/808/14949	Objection to voters 1753.
ARM. 5/2/1–17	Freeholders' Lists1813 to 1832.
T/808/14934	Freeholders' Registers 1830 to 1839.
T/808/14961	Freeholders' List 1839.
T/808/14927	Voters' List 19851.
D/1928/F/1–103	Freeholders' Registers, early 18th century to 1830.
D/671/2/5–6	Poll book, Co Down (part of) 1852.
D/671/2/7–8	Poll book Co Down (part of) 1857.

Co Down
DOW. 5/3/1&2	Registers of Freeholders 1777, 1780–95.
D/654/A3/1B	'Deputy Court Cheque Book' Freeholders' Register 1789.
T/393/1	Freeholders' List (Lecale barony only) c.1790.
D/654/A3/1	Freeholders' Registers 1813 to 1821: 1824.
T/761/19&20	Freeholders' Lists c.1830.

Co Fermanagh
T/808/15063	Poll Book 1747–63.
T/1385	Poll Book 1788.
T/543	Poll Book 1788.
T/808/15075	Poll book 1788.
D/1096/90	Freeholders' Registers 1796 to 1802.

Co Londonderry
T/2123	Freeholders' Registers (names A to L only) c.1813.
T/1048/1–4	City of Londonderry voters' list 1832.
D/1935/6	City of Londonderry voters' list 1868.
D/834/1	Freeholders' Register, City and County of Londonderry c.1840.

Co Tyrone
TYR5/3/1   Freeholders' list (Dungannon barony only) 1795–98.

Belfast
D/2472   Poll Book for Belfast 1832 to 1837.
BELF5/1/1/1–2   Register of Electors, Belfast 1855 and 1876.

After 1880, voters' lists are to be found in the Crown and Peace Records for the counties. For Cavan, the poll book for 1761 is in PRONI. Freeholders 1813–21 are listed in the National Library, NL Ir. 94119 c 2. Donegal free-holders, from 1761 to 1775, are in the National Library NL P.975, the Genealogical Office GO MS 442 and PRONI T/808/14999. The largest collection of surviving electoral registers is in the National Archives, though that is incomplete for many areas.

DOWNPATRICK TOWN SURVEY 1708

A survey of the town of Downpatrick was done, in that year, by James Maguire. He described each premises by name and gave its size, principal tenant and the half-yearly rent due. In 1927, the Rev David Stewart made a manuscript copy of this survey, which is available in PRONI, ref. D/1759/2A/8.

LIST OF PROTESTANT HOUSEHOLDERS 1740

This was done for parts of Antrim, Armagh, Derry, Down, Donegal and Tyrone. Arranged by county, barony and parish, it gives the names only. A typescript copy can be found on the shelves of the search room at PRONI. It can also be seen, at the Genealogical Office, for the parishes of Clonmeny, Culdaff, Desertegney, Donagh, Fawne, Moville and Templemore, ref. GO539. Copies can also be seen in the National Library, the Genealogical Office and the Representative Church Body Library.

CONVERT ROLLS 1703–1838

The Convert Rolls (Irish Manuscripts Commission, 1981) edited by Eileen O'Byrne in the National Library, gives a list of those converting from Roman Catholicism to the Church of Ireland. Most of the entries are for the period from 1760 to 1790. This is not, however, a comprehensive list.

RELIGIOUS CENSUS OF 1766

This was ordered by the government to be done, in March and April of that

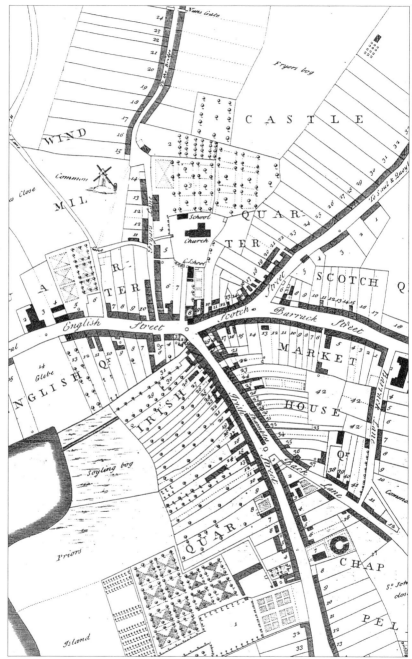

A detail from an 18th-century map of Downpatrick, Co Down. (Linen Hall Library)

year, by the parochial clergy of the Established Church. The resolution, passed in the Irish House of Lords, prescribed

> that the several archbishops and bishops of this kingdom shall be and are hereby desired to direct the parish ministers in their respective dioceses to return a list of the several families to the House on the first Monday after the recess, distinguishing which are Protestants and which are Papists, and also a list of the several reputed Popish priests and friars residing in their parishes.

The returns were arranged in alphabetical order, within each diocese, and stamped with a running number. The intention was to discover the religious persuasions of the population at large. Heads of households were listed, their religion and numbers of children. There was a great variation in the approach of the clergy to the census. Some listed every townland and householder, while others only gave numerical totals of the population. This led to considerable variance in the census, from parish to parish, and puts limits on its comparative use. Also, the gap between it and the next similar survey, contained in the Tithe Applotment Books, is 60 years. The other drawback is that it was largely destroyed in the Four Courts in 1922. What fragments have remained, have been augmented by transcripts, notably those made by Tenison Groves. In PRONI, transcript copies can be found on the search room shelves, ref. T/808/15264–15267. A full listing of all transcripts and abstracts is available on the open shelves of the reading rooms of the National Archives in Dublin.

ARMAGH CENSUS 1770

This gave individual names and occupations, size of family and religion, in the city. It is arranged street by street, PRONI ref. T/808/14938 and T/808/14977.

SPINNING-WHEEL PREMIUM ENTITLEMENT LISTS 1796

This entitlement was introduced to encourage the linen industry. Free spinning-wheels or looms were introduced to individuals who planted a certain area with flax. The lists, amounting to almost 60,000 individuals, recorded only the names of the individuals and the parish in which they lived. Over 64 per cent of the beneficiaries were in Ulster, where the industry was widespread and the list is a useful guide to its state at local level. Only those counties with over 3,000 names appear. Thus Antrim, Cavan and Fermanagh are absent from the county-by-county source lists, while Donegal has most names with over 14,000 recipients of the premium. At PRONI, a microfilm index to the lists, ref. T/3419 is available as is a typescript copy, on the search room shelves. There is a copy, on microfiche, in the National Archives. There are copies in the Linen Hall Library, Belfast and the Irish Linen Centre/Lisburn Museum. Local libraries may hold some lists for their areas.

4

NINETEENTH-CENTURY RECORDS

STATISTICAL SURVEYS OF THE ROYAL DUBLIN SOCIETY

The society was founded in 1750 as the Dublin Society for Promoting Husbandry and Other Useful Arts (from 1820, Royal Dublin Society). It was patronised by innovative and improving landlords and men of science and the arts of the Ascendancy class. It received grants from parliament, indicative of the importance of its work. The surveys were accounts of the social and economic aspects of rural life, with accompanying statistics, maps and projections for the future. They included descriptions of the main features of the landscape, often delivered more in the language of literature than of science. The statistical surveys were done by various authors and their quality varies accordingly. They can be consulted in the National Library of Ireland and other main libraries. This extract from pages 60–1 of the *Statistical survey of Donegal 1802*, by James McParlan, gives a flavour of its content.

Nature of Manures

From Donegal to Ballyshannon and Killybegs, sea-weed, shelly sand and dung are the manures; and although this tract abounds with limestone and lime-gravel, very little if any use is made of them. All through the immense mountain region of this county, paring, burning, and liming are neglected, sea-wrack and a scanty supply of dung are their only manures. Mr. Stewart of Ards, uses dung and composts of lime and scouring of ditches; sometimes lime, and till for reclaiming mountain, which it does with admirable effect, and in great quantities; and this practice begins to diffuse itself among the poor natives of his district . . . The Rev. Mr. Kennedy uses lime judiciously in reclaiming bog, and his exertions have induced numbers of the country people to follow his example, who were before strangers to the use of it.

For Ulster counties (none exists for Fermanagh), the statistical surveys extant are listed in Table 5.

Table 5: Ulster statistical surveys

County	Author	Date of compilation
Antrim	Dubourdieu	1812
Armagh	Dubourdieu	1804
Cavan	Coote	1802
Derry	Sampson	1802
Donegal	McParlan	1802
Down	Dubourdieu	1802
Monaghan	Coote	1801
Tyrone	McEvoy	1802

The Co Tyrone survey, *County Tyrone, 1802*, by John McAvoy, was reprinted by Friar's Bush Press (Belfast, 1991).

GRAND JURY PRESENTMENT BOOKS AND RECORDS

The Grand Jury system was an early form of local government, at county level providing the best source of records on the county prior to local government reform in 1898. Representation on the Grand Jury was by selection of the high sheriff and was usually confined to local landlords, their agents and lawyers. Their major responsibility was the levying of a county rate, which was cess-raised to further road-building. Grand Juries derived their powers from statutes of 1759 and 1765. The Juries heard requests for funds for projects such as road-building. The Presentment Books and Grand Warrants recorded the 'presentment' or allocation of county funds to particular baronies. They were usually arranged by barony within the county. They are important sources for dating the construction of roads, bridges and other related features such as settlement and field boundaries.

Grand Juries were also in charge of the building and maintenance of workhouses, dispensaries and lunatic asylums. As well, they often saw to the preparation of county maps. They could be responsible for some provision of social welfare and paying for the night watch. The complexity of local government requirements, in the late 19th century, resulted in the winding up of Grand Juries as part of the Irish Local Government Act of 1898. The name of these bodies still survives in some local place-names, such as Old Grand Jury Road, on the Crossgar side of Saintfield, Co Down. Grand Jury Presentment Records are in PRONI, for the area now covered by Northern Ireland and, in the National Archives, (with gaps) for Donegal 1805–99.

They are not indexed. Although frequently printed, different sets contain manuscript amendments and notes according to who owned and used them.

COUNTY OF DOWN.

TAKE NOTICE,

THAT APPLICATION will be made at the first Special Road Sessions, to be holden in **SAINTFIELD**, for the Barony of Upper Castlereagh, on the 10th day of **MAY** next, and at the ensuing Assizes, to widen, amend, and where necessary, to deviate from the Road from Saintfield to Downpatrick. Such improvements to commence at or near Laverty's School-house, in the Townland of Drumnaconnell, and thence through the following Townlands :— Drumnaconnell, 16 perches; Leggygowan, 381; Lisowen, 310; Clontinaglare, 117; Creevycarnonan, 630; Lissara, 34; in all 1488 perches, statute measure, in the Barony of Upper Castlereagh aforesaid. Such line not to be more than 32 feet wide in the clear, as per Maps, Plans, and Sections, lodged in the Office of the Secretary of the Grand Jury of the County aforesaid.

To all *Whom it* } may concern. }   16th *April*, 1841.

DOWNPATRICK: PRINTED AT THE RECORDER OFFICE.

Notice relating to road improvements in Co Down, 1841. (Linen Hall Library)

A typical entry might state 'that it,was agreed that £12. 6s. 8d. shall be paid to Joshua Trainor of Ballylack, for repairing the road between Omagh and Strabane, from Peter McMenamin's farm in Breeny to William Crawford's farm at Ballykilbeg'.

The most useful Grand Jury records in PRONI are listed below:

Co Antrim
ANT/4/1	Presentments 1711–1840 (typed extracts, 1711–21, are available on the shelves of the public search room).
ANT/4/2	Grand Warrant Books.
ANT/4/3	Presentments Books, working copies, 1822–99.
ANT/ 41/ 6	Grand Jury Book, 1849–1941.
ANT/4/8111	Booklet listing names of judges and high sheriffs, 1859–1900.
ANT/4/8/3	List of magistrates giving names, addresses and dates of appointment, 1873–1923.
T/1110	Grand Jury lists for Co Antrim, 1613–1803.

Co Armagh
ARM/41/1	Presentments 1758–1899.
ARM/4/2/1	County Cess Collection Book for the barony of Oneilland West, 1875.
T/647	Grand Jury List for Co Armagh, 1735–1797.

MASON'S PAROCHIAL SURVEY OF IRELAND

William Shaw Mason, secretary to the Board of Records, organised a survey, by the clergy of the established church, of each parish, under a list of headings, including 'the name of the parish ancient and modern, its situation, extent and divisions, climate and topographical description'. They were also asked to make suggestions for improvements in the situation of the people. The survey was published in three volumes, in the years 1814, 1816 and 1819. As it depended on the diligence of individual clergy, it varied from place to place and was often sparse in its information. In all, only 79 parishes were surveyed. In Ulster the parishes listed in Table 6 were included. Relevant copies may be found in local libraries.

Table 6: Mason's parochial survey

Parish or union	Diocese	County
Vol I (1814)		
Ahoghill	Connor	Antrim
Ballintoy	Connor	Antrim
Dunaghy	Connor	Antrim
Finvoy	Connor	Antrim
Creggan	Armagh	Armagh
Baillieborough	Kilmore	Cavan
Clomanny (Clonmany)	Derry	Donegal
Dungiven	Derry	Derry
Kilbarron	Raphoe	Donegal
Maghera	Derry	Derry
Templecarne	Clogher	Fermanagh/Donegal
Vol II (1816)		
Aghalee	Dromore	Antrim
Glenavy	Connor	Antrim
Ramoan	Connor	Antrim
Ballymoyer	Armagh	Armagh
Seagoe	Armagh	Armagh
Culdaff	Derry	Donegal
Cloncha	Derry	Donegal
Inver	Derry	Donegal
Annahilt	Dromore	Down
Devenish	Clogher	Fermanagh
Vol III (1819)		
Ardclinis &c.	Connor	Antrim
Killelagh	Derry	Derry
Tamlaght	Armagh	Derry and Tyrone
Holywood	Down	Down
Errigall-keroge	Armagh	Tyrone

NINETEENTH-CENTURY PARLIAMENTARY PAPERS (BLUE BOOKS)

In the 19th century, as society became more complex and the administration of Ireland more bureaucratic, a huge volume of records was generated from state sources. These provide a greater amount of material for the local historian than had been the case in previous centuries. For the period from the Act of Union to 1921, one of the principal sources for local studies are the Parliamentary Papers, often termed 'Blue Books'. Many of these publications, such as reports of parliamentary committees and commissions, have substantial material of a purely local nature included in minutes of evidence and appendices. Also, parliament published a wide variety of accounts and statistics each year, many of which are tabulated in a manner which presents regional and local data in a readily accessible form. The 'returns' were the documents printed in response to requests for information from the House of Commons. The other type is the annual report of government departments or other official bodies. However, for the period in question, there were over 7,000 volumes published and to find those with data on a particular locality involves much searching through indexes. *Ireland in the Nineteenth Century: A Breviate of Official Publications*, A and J Maltby, London, 1979, is particularly useful as it gives summaries of the more important publications. Well over 600 papers have been summarised and arranged into 12 broad classes. The Maltbys were at one stage librarians at Queen's University, Belfast. The Parliamentary Papers are available in Queen's University Library and in the National Library of Ireland. Small collections of Parliamentary Papers are held in each of the area board library headquarters and also in the county libraries at Clones and Letterkenny. The following are examples of Parliamentary Papers with substantial data for most parts of the country, here arranged under broad subject categories. The volume number, where given, is a National Library reference.

The following relates to the condition of the people:
- Reports of Commissioners for enquiring into the condition of the poorer classes in Ireland, 1835, Vol XXXII, Pts 1–2; 1836, Vols XXXI–XXXIV have data on housing clothing, rent, employment, wages, emigration: compiled on the basis of information supplied by priests, ministers and justices of the peace. *His Majesty's Commissioners for Inquiring into the Condition of the Poorer Classes in Ireland, Reports and Appendices*, in HCP, 1835, xxxii, part 1; 1836, xxx–xxxiv; 1837, li; 1837–38, xxxviii; 1845, xliii (index) gives a detailed account of poverty in Ireland, prior to the introduction of the Poor Law. Its appendices contain individual reports of many towns and parishes. Papers relating to the proceedings for the relief of distress and to the state of the unions and workhouses in Ireland:

mainly in House of Commons Papers; 1846, Vol XXXVII; 1847, Vols L–LV; 1847–8, Vols LIV–LVI; 1849, Vol XLVIII (include correspondence and associated papers from relief committees officials, priests, landlords and others, and documents relating to workhouse and relief adminis-tration). In the parliamentary papers, these are the main reports on the state of the country in terms of deprivation and the working of the Poor Law.

• The second major report is *The Vice-Regal Commission on Poor Law Reform in Ireland 1906*. Its minutes of evidence contain some information for every area and its appendix contains statistics for all unions. The annual reports of the overall supervisory bodies namely the Poor Law Commissioners 1839–47, the Poor Law Commission For Ireland 1842–72 and the Local Government Board for Ireland 1872–1921, show the changes in provision over the years. All contain reports, maps and statistics relating to local unions.

The following relate to land and agrarian crime:
• Report of Select Committee on the draining of bogs in Ireland. 1810, Vol X (paper no 365); 1810–11, Vol Vl (paper no 96); 1813–14, Vol VI, Pts 1–2 (gives details of proprietors, turf-cutting, valuation, reclamation, roads; with maps and surveys).
• Minutes of evidence before the Select Committee appointed to enquire into the disturbances in Ireland, 1825, Vols V11–IX (investigation of crime resulting from agrarian and tithe grievances; with detailed topographical index).
• Report from the Select Committee on the state of Ireland, 1831–32, Vol XVI (includes minutes of evidence).
• Report of Commissioners of Inquiry into the state of the law and practice in respect of the occupation of land in Ireland (Devon Commission 1845), Vols XIX–XXII (includes evidence given at sessions held throughout the country; information on relations between landlord and tenant, distress, emigration consolidation; on average about 30 persons gave evidence from each county so all areas are represented).
• Report of Commission on Landlord and Tenant Act, 1870 (Bessborough Commission), 1881, Vols XVIII–XIX.
• Report of the Evicted Tenants Commission, 1893–94, Vol XXXI

The following concerns towns and commerce:
• Evidence before Select Committee on the tolls and customs at markets and fairs in Ireland, 1834, Vol XVII.
• Reports of Commissioners on the state of fairs and markets in Ireland, 1852–53, Vol XLI; 1854–55, Vol XIX (include lists of places and dates of

fairs and markets with information on patents, systems of weighing and bargaining, amenities).
- Reports of Commissioners on the state of the municipal corporations in Ireland, 1835, Vols XXVII–XXVIII; 1836, Vol XXIV (include history of each town corporation with details of charters and powers).
- Reports of Commissioners appointed to consider and recommend a general system of railways for Ireland, 1837, Vol XXXIII; 1837–38, Vol XXXV.

The following concerns education:
- Reports from the Commissioners of the Board of Education in Ireland, 1813–14, Vol V (has lists and details of diocesan free schools, parish schools, Royal Schools, classical schools and a variety of similar institutions).
- Commissioners of Irish Education Inquiry, second report, 1826–27, Vol XII, Pts 1–2 (has list of all schools, including hedge-schools arranged by parish; for each school it gives the number and religious denomination of pupils; the names, religion and income of teachers; description of the schoolhouse).
- Commissioners of Public Instruction in Ireland, second report, 1835, Vols XXXIII–XXXIV (also has data showing the developments over the interim period). It contains data based largely on clerical reports of church attendance.
- Reports of Select Committee on foundation schools and education in Ireland, 1837–8, Vol VII (has data on diocesan free schools, charter schools and similar institutions).
- Reports of Commissioners on the state of the endowed schools in Ireland 1857–8, Vol XXII, Pts 1–4 (has information on physical and academic aspects of the schools and on the administration of endowments including landed estates).
- Return from schools in Ireland showing those receiving grants from the National Education Commissioners; listing the mixed and unmixed, the number on roll and average attendance; the number, religion and classification of teachers, amounts received by teachers from the National Education Commissioners and received by the school from local aid, 1892, Vol LX.

POPULATION SURVEYS AND CENSUSES

The most accurate way of gauging the population, its make-up and changing nature, both locally and nationally, is the census. The earliest official census in Ireland was done, between 1813 and 1815, but not for the whole country. Much more comprehensive censuses were done in 1821 and 1831. Both were organised by townland, civil parish, barony and county and, although they are not totally accurate, can give an overview of population trends. Only a few volumes of the original manuscripts survive for Ulster, relating to Co Fermanagh, PRONI ref. MIC 5A and MIC 15A. For 1831, which includes questions on name, age, occupation and religion, the only surviving fragmented records in PRONI relate to Co Londonderry. The references for these are:

MIC 5A/6	Barony of Coleraine
MIC 5A/6 and 7	City of Londonderry
MIC 5A/8	Barony of Loughlinsholim
MIC 5A/9	Barony of Tirkeeran

From 1841, the census statistics are available in published form on a decennial basis. The census of that and succeeding years is much more worthy of attention. Certainly 1841 is extremely important as the only reliable and comprehensive pre-Famine census, taken when the population of the country as a whole was approaching a peak from which it would be dramatically and tragically diminished. These changes can be indicated by correlation with post-Famine statistics. The 1841 census was of a higher order of efficiency because the enumerators were mainly police personnel and also due to the availability of the first edition of 6-inch OS maps. Unfortunately none of the census enumerators' reports for what is now Northern Ireland have survived. The results though are available, PRONI ref. T/550.

The territorial divisions used were province, county, barony, civil parish, town and townland. The definition of town as being a group of 20 or more houses created an exaggerated picture of the degree of urbanisation, although this was to change. The fact that figures for individual townlands were given is of great value to the local historian. In this respect also, the classification of houses, according to size and condition, is a boon. Thus, class 4 was a mud cabin with one room; class 3 again a mud cabin with two to three rooms and windows; class 2, a good farm house or town house, had five to nine rooms and windows. The class 1 house was classified as superior to the rest. One caution, about these classifications, is that they were the work of individual enumerators and consequently the degree of uniformity applied over a region is open to question. This can have consequences for comparative studies such as the level of poverty from one area to another.

Another aspect of the census, of particular interest to the rural historian, is the collation of agricultural statistics, which was a secondary part of the enumerator's role. This agricultural census is regarded as somewhat unreliable in the early years especially as the use of the measure of statute acres or Irish acres (= 1.6 statute acres) was a matter of the preference of the enumerator. This may have helped to create an exaggerated picture of the Irish agricultural norm as the small-holding of under five acres. The fact that large areas of waste-land were often not recorded as part of the farm also artificially reduced the recorded size of holdings. The census also recorded land use, ie the extent of arable and non-arable land, livestock and other farm produce. Statistics were also given for education and literacy. This was important in terms of state planning for the new national education system. For historians, looking at change in the locality due to famine and emigration, the decennial census statistics are a *sine qua non* in terms of the changes in families and individuals residing in an area.

An important innovation was the census maps, four in total, showing:

1. Population density per square mile and population of towns.
2. 'The proportion of every 100 persons who occupy fourth class accommodation'. This was important in the growing debate on deprivation.
3. 'The proportion of every 100 persons who can neither read nor write'.
4. 'The value of stock to each 100 acres'. The importance of these maps is that they are veritable snapshots of Ireland and its regions which at a glance render accessible rather complex statistical concepts.

As the original detailed census enumeration returns for those years remain only in fragmentary form, they could be supplemented with parish registers in the relatively few areas where these are extant. Unfortunately earlier censuses have largely been vandalised in one way or another. Most of the censuses from 1841–91 were either pulped for wastepaper, in the First World War and earlier, or destroyed in the Four Courts in the Civil War in 1922. It is therefore to the censuses of 1901 and 1911 that local historians must turn as the earliest complete surviving records. The fact that enumeration books are closed to the public for 100 years (in Northern Ireland) nevertheless leaves us with the still considerable abstracts of data. While this rule has been dropped in the National Archives, including the data referring to the six counties of Northern Ireland, they remain closed in PRONI until 2001 and 2011. In Ireland, the records for 1901 and 1911 compiled by the enumerators are not in books but in loose forms. The 1901 census in PRONI, reference number MIC/354, is on microfilm. The 1901 census is arranged by poor law union, electoral division, county, barony, parish, townland street if in a town or city.

The uses for this data are manifold. The townland is of course the basic unit for most local research. Each townland can be identified in the Topographical Index of 1904 based on the 1901 census, which was also done for the 1851 and 1871 censuses. As well as towns and townlands, it lists parishes, baronies, poor law unions, district electoral divisions, dispensary or registrars' districts, county districts, county electoral divisions, county and borough parliamentary divisions. It is a useful tool for locating a particular

townland. Detailed statistics, other than the basic population totals and numbers of houses, were not given as there were c.65,000 townlands in Ireland in
1901. Thus it is to the groups of townlands, in wider administrative units,
such as district electoral divisions (DED), registration districts and dispensary districts (relevant to workhouse dispensary entitlement), that the
researcher must turn to extract details about ages, education levels, religion
and Irish-speakers. The townland classification of the household returns of
each townland or street are grouped together in alphabetical order and the
returns of each arranged alphabetically. Indexes for each county are available
from which microfilm copies of the original returns may be brought up.

Each original set of household returns, for a townland or street, first gives
aggregate details in abstract of the houses and their occupants thus:
addresses by name of head of household; valuation criteria for each house,
including building materials; number of rooms and windows; the number
and type of outbuildings for each house, an abstract of the gender, religious
denomination and number of persons in each household and the entire set.
Family returns comprise personal information on names and surnames of
each family member; their relationship to the head of household; religious
denomination; literacy level; age, sex, occupation, marital status; county of
birth or country if outside Ireland; ability to speak English or Irish and dis-
abilities if any. In 1911, married women additionally had to give information
on the number of children born alive and still living. Often in practice
widows also gave this information.

Of course, what use researchers make of this material is dependent on
their research aims or interests. The range of research that can be encom-
passed by census data is broad. Further information, on using census material, can be found in an article by Brenda Collins, 'The analysis of census
returns: the 1901 Census of Ireland' in *Ulster Local Studies*, vol 15, no 1,
Summer 1993 and also in R Breen, 'Population trends in late nineteenth and
early twentieth century Ireland: a local study', *The Economic and Social
History Review*, vol 15, no 2, January 1984.

POOR LAW RECORDS

The Ordnance Survey was set up to restructure local taxation and was
already in operation when the Poor Law was devised on the English model
following the survey of 1836. The Poor Law system, introduced into Ireland
in 1838, set up Boards of Poor Law Guardians (PLG) to administer relief to
the poor. At first, there was only to be 'indoor relief' provided in workhouses.
However the destitution arising from the Famine overwhelmed the system
and resulted in the granting of outdoor relief to the able-bodied poor in the
form of money or goods. Thus, those who entered workhouses tended to be

the old, very young or sick. Ireland was divided into some 137 Poor Law administrative districts, known as unions, based on market towns, each with their own workhouses and each generating records. This was fortunate for the historian, if not always for the destitute poor. The workhouse had an infirmary and fever hospital attached. The financing of this system came from a rate collected under the Poor Law Valuation. This valuation also made necessary the Ordnance Survey and Valuation of Ireland.

The records relating to the Poor Law consist mainly of the PLG minute books, admission and discharge registers, births and deaths registers and outdoor relief registers. All of these are of interest in terms of the fate of people in the locality. The tally of admission records and payment of outdoor relief measure fluctuations in the level of distress in a given area or indeed in a particular trade or occupation. Guardian minutes are also a good indication of the attitude of the middle and upper classes towards the less well-off. For example, the chairman of the Belfast Guardians, Lily Coleman, during a 1929 board meeting, referring to what she regarded as the over-large families of the poor, stated, 'There is no poverty under the blankets!' (Linen Hall Library Belfast Book Collection 1929). The infirmary and fever hospital records are useful for a medical history and particularly in plotting epidemic patterns. The records of different unions provide excellent material for comparative area studies. This is particularly important, prior to the local government reform of 1898, when boards of guardians were often the only local government authority in many villages and small towns. The minute books also record the names of individuals whom the board of guardians assisted to emigrate.

There were 27 unions in the six counties of what is now Northern Ireland and 43 in Ulster as a whole. In PRONI, the printed Valuation Books of 1860 (on the shelves of the public search room) are organised on the basis of Union districts, thus enabling us to identify, through the board records, the townland or parish we are interested in. The unions were named after a chief town and often districts extended across counties and the present border. The records are closed for 100 years from the latest date in each volume.

The Northern Ireland records can be traced through the grey calendars on the PRONI public search room shelves, with the following references.

BG1   Antrim
BG2   Armagh
BG3   Ballycastle
BG4   Ballymena
BG5   Ballymoney
BG6   Banbridge
BG7   Belfast, counties Antrim and Down

BG8   Castlederg
BG9   Clogher
BG10   Coleraine
BG11   Cookstown
BG12   Downpatrick
BG13   Dungannon
BG14   Enniskillen
BG15   Irvinestown
BG16   Kilkeel
BG17   Larne
BG18   [Newton] Limavady
BG19   Lisburn
BG20   Lisnaskea
BG21   Londonderry
BG22   Lurgan
BG23   Magherafelt
BG24   Newry
BG25   Newtownards
BG26   Omagh
BG27   Strabane
BG28   Gortin (united to Omagh, c.1870)

There are a number of PLG records in PRONI for counties Donegal and Monaghan (Carrickmacross BG56 and Castleblayney BG51). The Poor Law records for Co Cavan are in the County Library in Cavan Town and for Donegal they are in the County Library, Lifford. In Co Monaghan the records for the Union of Castleblayney are in the Ballybay branch library. See also the Irish Famine Network publication *Records of the Irish Famine*, D Lindsay and D Fitzpatrick (Dublin, 1993), pp 1–29.

The records of the Ministry of Home Affairs 1921–48, continue the story of the unions in Northern Ireland until their replacement by the post-war welfare state. The stigma of the Poor Law still remains in folk memory. For example, some old people still refuse to go into the City Hospital in Belfast for fear that they should die in what was once the workhouse.

The following are extracts from the rough minutes of the Enniskillen Board of Guardians, PRONI ref. BGXIV/A/1, at the time of the Famine. They graphically illustrate the overwhelming of the facilities of the work-house by hunger and disease.

19 January 1847
Proposed by Edward Archdale Esquire and seconded by Captain Corry resolved that a communication be addressed to the Poor Law Commissioners to the following effect: the extraordinary increase of paupers admitted into the

Workhouse during the existence of the calamity which inflicts the country has involved the establishment in considerable debt, say to the contractors . . . Under these circumstances some of the contractors have refused further supplies and unless funds be raised for the present expenditure the Guardians will be obliged, however painful to their feelings, to close the Workhouse and put out the unfortunate paupers . . . Resolved that as the Rt. Hon. Earl of Enniskillen is fortunately at present in Dublin, and being aware of his great anxiety for the welfare of the Union he be requested to have the goodness to communicate the resolution of the Board now adopted to the Lord Lieutenant and to use his influence with his Excellency in order that the Union may be relieved from the awful calamity with which it is threatened.

14 September 1847
Resolved that the Clerk be directed to notice the Guardians for next meeting to take into consideration how the burial account is to be charged in the last half year's accounts as the registry of death was not properly kept in consequence of the deaths of so many of the officers . . .

VALUATION RECORDS

The valuation of property to introduce rates to pay for the administration of the Poor Law has consequently provided us with a wealth of local information. In PRONI the valuation records are for the area covered by Northern Ireland, 1830s–1975. There is a series of valuations and revaluations, 1830s, 1854–64, 1864–1929, 1935, 1956, 1975 and a special re-evaluation of Belfast in the early years of the 20th century. In 1826 a valuation act replaced the old Grand Jury system of levying rates for local government expenditure, which had been in place from an act of 1635. Sir Richard Griffith (1784–1878), Commissioner of the General Survey and Valuation of Rateable Property in Ireland, was appointed in 1827, and the valuations of 1854–64 are called after him. The printed version of these valuation records is available in the public search room of PRONI. Griffith also worked for the Ordnance Survey, being an engineer by profession. He had a great interest in geology and has been dubbed 'the father of Irish geology'.

The earliest was the Townland Valuation of the 1830s which, as its name indicates, took the townland as the unit for valuation. These records consist of some 500 field books (VAL/1B) and corresponding maps (VAL/1A) on a scale of 6 inches to 1 mile and town maps (VAL/1D) scale 60 inches to 1 mile. The need for maps for valuation purposes led to the setting up of the Ordnance Survey for Ireland (OS) under Lt Col Thomas Colby (see pp 42–6). These maps were to become the standard for official use. The first of Griffith's townland valuations was of Coleraine, begun in May 1830, using Colby's base maps.

This and the subsequent valuations and revaluations are of particular value to local historians as they describe and evaluate each area in precise detail that is nowhere else available. The changes, that have been made in each locality, are recorded in ways that allow a longitudinal study. In the first valuation, it was the townland and the more substantial houses, at a required valuation of £5, that were valued. Industrial and commercial buildings were also valued and the field books are important sources for the location and description of important industrial sites in the 1830s.

In the second survey, generally known as Griffith's Valuation, the Primary Valuation of Ireland, a valuation was made of all individual properties. This was necessitated by the Poor Relief Act (Ireland) which required such valuation for striking the poor rate. It was known officially as the First Tenement Valuation 1846–64. The printed volumes of this are found on the shelves of the public search room arranged by Poor Law Union, within union by county, and then into parishes and townlands. The original notebooks (VAL/2B), comprehensively indexed, contain details about buildings, etc. The main headings included the number of the property, occupier, immediate lessor (usually the chief landlord for the area), description of the tenement, area of the property, and valuation of buildings and lands. Other properties, for example, schools, railway stations and churches, though exempt from valuation, are included, as are topographical notes.

Revision lists 1865–1929 (VAL/12B)

These are available as annual revision lists in 10-year volumes. Changes in properties were recorded in different colours of ink for each year. Thus comparisons can be made of valuation revisions over the years. Whereas all townlands are included in the series from 1864 to 1929–30, the changes in administrative boundaries may mean a change from one volume to another. The parish or union can be traced through the Topographical Index, in the public search room, which is an alphabetically arranged list of all the townlands in Ireland, compiled since the 1851 census.

Maps to accompany tenement valuation 1858–1929

Each property valued was shown on an OS map known as a valuation map. Griffith's valuation maps have the reference number VAL/2D and are arranged alphabetically by counties. Town valuation maps were done in the 1830s (VAL/1D) and in the years 1858–64 (VAL/2D), and 1864–1935 (VAL/12E) This last series, covering some 200 towns and villages, is a particularly useful source on town life in the early part of this century. This tenement valuation was kept under continuous review with dated annotations in coloured ink so that it was straightforward to discover the changing settlement pattern of a townland or street.

PRONI have issued the following instructions in their leaflet *Your Family Tree 20: How to Use Griffith's Valuation*:

1. Use the Householders Index to find in which county the name is most prevalent.
2. Having done this the Householders Index will indicate in which barony/parish the name is most often found.
3. At the start of each parish there will be information to tell you which union the parish is in, eg Lisburn Union, Co Antrim.
4. The relevant union book will list the pages for the required barony/parish and the townlands therein.
5. Search the pages of the barony/parish for the required name. The details shown beside the name will indicate the type of property, acreage and valuation.
6. The numbers to the left of the name are the plot numbers and relate to a particular valuation map. The start of the townland states which map is needed.
7. The valuation maps are listed as follows:

VAL.2A/1/ sheet number   Co Antrim.
VAL.2A/2/ sheet number   Co Armagh.
VAL.2A/3/ sheet number   Co Down.
VAL.2A/4/ sheet number   Co Fermanagh.
VAL.2A/5/ sheet number   Co Londonderry.
VAL.2A/6/ sheet number   Co Tyrone.

Maps should be ordered by county and sheet number as indicated at the start of the townland.

Records, this century, have concerned the Revaluation of Belfast 1900–06, Northern Ireland General Revaluations 1935–54 (Val/3) and 1956–72 (Val/4). The latter contains war-damage files. A computerised geographical index, available in the foyer of PRONI, allows the researcher to key in any townland name and access its relevant valuation references. The researcher is fortunate to have such records for areas as specific as townlands, which are at the kernel of Irish local history. Valuation records as a whole, taken in tandem with other sources, such as the census and local directories, can be used to construct a detailed picture of each area, from the middle of last century, to the recent past. An important work on using Griffith's Valuation with parish registers is *A Guide to Parish Registers* (Baltimore USA, 1988) by Brian Mitchell. An excellent article giving all the above information and more is 'Valuation records in the Public Records Office of Northern Ireland', *Ulster Local Studies*, vol 16, no 2, Winter 1994, by Trevor Parkhill. Consultation of the article would pay dividends to those intending to use valuation records in PRONI.

THE ORDNANCE SURVEY OF IRELAND

The Ordnance Survey (OS) was set up in Ireland in the autumn of 1824. It came about as a result of a parliamentary commission report which the Prime Minister, the Duke of Wellington accepted. The primary purpose of the OS was to provide maps for the valuation of Ireland to support the local taxation system (county cess), which gave way to the new Poor Law regime. It was carried out by Royal Engineer officers and three companies of sappers and miners, under the command of Colonel Thomas Colby (1784–1852). Also, civil servants and scholars were assigned to help with sketching, drawing and engraving maps and writing accompanying descriptive accounts (see pp 46–9). The OS produced maps and plans on a variety of scales ranging from 10 miles to the inch to 1/500. The survey at 6 inch to the mile provided the valuation office with maps on a scale large enough to show townland boundaries. Ireland was the first country to be completely mapped on such a large scale. The first edition of the 6-inch survey was published between 1833 and 1846. While this is the best known and most used, other smaller-scale topographical maps were produced, such as the ¼ inch, ½ inch and 1 inch; the 6 inch and 25 inch plans and the large-scale town plans, usually at 1/1056 and 1/500.

The team of highly-skilled army engineers was led for 20 years by Colby. The survey began in 1830 with the map of the city of Derry. The first base line, from which most subsequent maps of Ireland have been produced, was an eight-mile stretch between Magilligan and Ballykelly. It was measured in 1828–30 with special compensating bars of Colby's invention. It was so accurate that modern measures have found it to be only 1 inch out. The maps are of interest to the local historian in many respects. First, the survey was begun at a time when the population of Ireland was at its highest and changes in density of settlement can be observed on subsequent maps. The 6-inch maps indicate the boundaries of counties, baronies, civil parishes and townlands. They show cities, towns, villages, estates, farms, manufactories, mines, churches, etc (see classification below). They record the antiquities of note in every area. They differentiate land as cultivated, uncultivated or bog. Again, changes are evident in successive maps.

PRONI has over 40,000 printed and manuscript OS maps, on various scales, which cover practically every foot of ground in Northern Ireland. Perhaps the most useful, for the local historian, is the county map on the scale of 6 inches to 1 statute mile (1:10560), each sheet covering 24 square miles. With successive editions, it is possible by comparison to trace continuity and change in a given area. Townland maps exist on this scale from 1842. Subsequent editions for Ulster were for 1853–61, 1903–06 and 1921–39 (fourth edition). Studies can thus be undertaken on patterns of development in many topics such as transport, industry, agriculture, field and natural boundaries and mineral resource sites. Industrial archaeology is well served by this kind of exercise. The OS maps are also useful sources for archaeological sites, place-names and schools before the National System of Education. Another interesting map for the study of a locality, is the much larger 25-inch scale.

A complete survey of the Ulster counties, in this much larger scale, became available at the turn of the century, for 1894–1904 and subsequently for 1920–24. The scale 1:1056 has been used for towns since the early 1860s. PRONI has maps for 24 Ulster towns on the scale of 1:5000, published c.1861, providing a very detailed record of those towns, which was subsequently used for valuation purposes. These maps can be seen in PRONI and some relevant copies can be obtained in the local libraries. This section has been a précis of an excellent article by Trevor Parkhill, 'Ordnance Survey maps in the Public Record Office of Northern Ireland' in *Ulster Local Studies*, vol 14, no 2.

The classification of map content
In the following example, the 6-inch series shows the range, depth and detail of information contained, though not all was on every map.

Boundaries: townlands, civil parishes, baronies, counties, municipalities, wards.

Topographical features: rivers, streams, lakes, waterfalls, rapids, cliffs, rock outcrops, hill tops, caves.

Vegetation features: fir plantation, mixed wood, brushwood, rocky heathy pasture, marsh, bog, furze, limit of cultivation.

Agricultural features: farm houses and buildings, field boundaries, blacksmiths, lime kilns, demesnes, orchards, gardens, plant nurseries, drainage channels, sluices, fish ponds.

Industrial features: factories, foundries, mills (corn, flour, flax, beetling, paper), windmills, ponds, bleach greens, ropeworks, tanneries, breweries, distilleries, quarries, sand and gravel pits, collieries, mines, brick fields, weirs and dams, millraces.

Settlement: towns, villages, fair grounds, public buildings, chapels (Roman Catholic and Presbyterian), churches, meeting houses, institutions, hospitals, workhouses, dispensaries, inns, wells, post offices, constabulary and

army barracks, alms houses, gasworks, graveyards, spas, race courses, bathing places, antiquities, (forts, raths, standing stones, moats, motes), ruined buildings.

Transport: roads, lanes, bridges, fords, canals and locks, aqueducts, railways and stations, ferries, harbours, piers, mooring posts.

Place-names: baronies, civil parishes, townlands, cities, towns, villages, bays and harbours, rivers, gentlemen's seats, bog names, loughs, woods, islands.

The place-names of the Ordnance Survey in many ways represent a compromise in linguistic terms which does not always accord with local usage. This was because there were many different variations of the same words from place to place. The OS employed linguistic experts to try to standardise and regularise these place-names, in an English form, most of them being Gaelic in origin. The man most associated with this aspect of the survey was John O'Donovan, who was born in the townland of Attatteemore in Co Kilkenny on 9 July 1809, and died on 9 December 1861. One of the foremost Gaelic scholars of his day, O'Donovan edited and translated the *Annals of the Four Masters* and published a grammar of Irish. He was a co-founder in 1840 of the Irish Archaeological Society. He later became the first Professor of Celtic at Queen's College, Belfast. O'Donovan was at considerable pains to stick as closely as possible to the original meaning and form of the place-names. It was very important to get this right as the place-names on the maps would become part of the legal process, not least in relation to valuation.

O'Donovan's ordnance survey work entailed travelling all over Ireland. Colonel Colby, his deputy Lieutenant Thomas Larcom and George Petrie, who had charge of antiquities in the OS headquarters, encouraged O'Donovan to observe and record antiquities, myths and legends and old Gaelic music, particularly in the remoter areas, before they were lost to posterity. Indeed the Famine and the subsequent clearances and emigration were to eradicate much of what O'Donovan recorded. Thus we are indebted to him for the enthusiastic and comprehensive way in which he carried out his brief. He sent back hundreds of letters to Phoenix Park, from all over Ireland, the originals of which are available in the Royal Irish Academy (RIA) in Dublin. These take up 50 volumes and are fortunately available to us in a typescript form transcribed by Fr Michael Flanagan. They provide astute and wide-ranging observations on the places and people he visited. *John O'Donovan's Letters From County Londonderry (1834)*, edited by Graham Mawhinney and published by Ballinascreen Historical Society in 1992, make them more accessible to people in that county. JB Cunningham, in his article, 'The letters of John O'Donovan in County Fermanagh: dogs, turkeycocks and ganders', in *Ulster Local Studies*, vol 14, no 2, also illustrates how useful these letters are to the local historian. He has now published this as a

John O'Donovan (1809–61), historian and Irish language scholar who made a major contribution to the recording of place-names for the Ordnance Survey in the early 19th-century. (National Gallery of Ireland)

volume. O'Donovan's letters to HQ provide an illuminating and often amusing picture of life in the island as a whole.

ORDNANCE SURVEY MEMOIRS

Another useful legacy, for the local historian, has been the Ordnance Survey Memoirs. Some would even see it as the starting point for any local study of pre-Famine Ulster. Lieutenant, later Sir, Thomas Larcom, who was appointed Colby's deputy in 1826, worked for the OS for more than 15 years at its headquarters in Phoenix Park. He was largely responsible for the memoirs which were furnished to the HQ, by the engineers and others working on the OS, along with the plans and maps. They give unique descriptions of pre-Famine Ulster in much more detail than could be contained in a census. These memoirs covered each parish, divided into townlands, and contained essential information which could not be fitted on to the maps or plans. They documented the topography, the built environment, land-holdings and population, employment and livelihood of the parishes. As well, they recorded the customs, habits, dress, food and drink of the people. The idea of submitting the memoirs, beginning from about 1830, was down to Colby, and the early memoirs and came largely from officers in the field and developed haphazardly at first. It was Larcom who decided to standardise what was proving a very useful exercise by issuing a 'Heads of Inquiry' guideline which codified the headings under which the memoirs were to be written. These are contained in a 37-page pamphlet of 1833 now in the National Library in Dublin, ref. Larcom Papers (LP) 7550.

Each Memoir was to be written under the following headings:

Section I: geography or natural state: (a) natural features: hills, lakes, rivers, bogs, woods, coast, climates; and (b) natural history: botany, zoology, geology.

Section II: topography or artificial state: 1. modern: towns, public buildings, gentlemen's seats, bleach greens, manufactures, mills, communications. 2. ancient: the history of the parish, as shown by objects of antiquity, and ancient buildings which remain. 3. general appearance and scenery.

Section III: the people or present state: 1. social economy: early improvements, local government, dispensaries, schools, poor, religion, habits of the people. 2. productive economy: occupations, manufactures and agriculture. (a) rural (b) commercial and manufacturing (c) possibilities for improvement.

Section IV: divisions of land: townlands

Appendix: tables of schools – occupations and the supporting statistical information.

The Heads of Inquiry resulted in the setting up of a separate department, within the Ordnance Survey, to compile the great amount of material coming in from the field. By 1840, when it was halted, over 15,000 pages of Memoir material been accumulated, in effect a huge social survey of the areas covered.

The scope of the memoirs can be elucidated from the instruction of one of Larcom's deputies, Captain, later Major-General, JE Portlock, to those under his command.

> . . . each person should note all he sees and all he hears, whether in reference to his own immediate inquiries, to the social condition and habits of the people, to antiquities and traditionary recollections of all kinds, or to natural history in all its branches, naming at the same time his authority for each statement.

The memoirs primarily covered the counties of Ulster, with only fragments for 10 other counties. The counties of Derry and Antrim were done most comprehensively, followed by Down, Fermanagh, Tyrone and Donegal. Armagh, Monaghan and Cavan were the least well recorded. The memoirs

Station Island, Lough Derg, Co Donegal. A drawing by Lt William Lancey of the Ordnance Survey, in the 1830s. An account of the Lough Derg pilgrimage can be found in Ordnance Survey Memoirs of Ireland, Vol 39, *Belfast 1997. (Royal Irish Academy)*

for counties Antrim and Derry also give lists of those who, due to economic depression combined with rising population, had emigrated to North America in the previous few years. The majority of those are described as having gone to Canada, though many subsequently moved on to the United States. Ulster local historians thus have a wonderfully comprehensive word-picture of life in the 1830s and 1840s, denied to their counterparts in the rest of the country. This is especially important in terms of studying localities prior to and after the Great Famine. The Memoir for only one parish was published by the time of the winding up of the scheme, that of Templemore on the west bank of Derry city and district, which came out in 1837. There is no memoir for Belfast/Shankill or Armagh City.

The fact that no other memoirs were subsequently published, left a gap, in the historiography of Ulster, which fortunately is now filled by the publication of the *Ordnance Survey Memoirs of Ireland* series, edited by Angélique Day and Patrick McWilliams, at the Institute of Irish Studies, the Queen's University of Belfast, in association with the Royal Irish Academy. The completed project comprises 40 volumes and a comprehensive place-name and personal-name index is currently under preparation. The series is a veritable Domesday book for the Ulster counties and indispensable to the local historian. The letters and name-books and many of the sketches of antiquities and interesting topographical features are not included in the published edited volumes of memoirs. However, these can be accessed, in their original form of some 600 manuscripts, in the Royal Irish Academy and National Archives in Dublin.

The memoirs project was wound up in 1840. This was occasioned by the curt message, from the Master of the Ordnance in England, to 'revert immediately to its original object under the valuation acts', namely to provide maps for the purpose of estimating a uniform and equitable valuation for the country and local rates. The reason for its cessation was mainly government retrenchment under Prime Minister Peel.

The original materials for the Ordnance Survey Memoirs are as follows. In the Royal Irish Academy, Dublin are the memoirs (boxes 1–52). The OS collection also includes letters, extracts, inquisitions, sketches and other miscellaneous documents. The memoirs for counties Antrim, Armagh, Cavan, Derry, Donegal, Down, Fermanagh, Monaghan and Tyrone, as well as for Queen's County, Roscommon, Sligo and Tipperary, are available on microfilm at PRONI, ref. MIC/6. This microfilm series includes 'name-books', containing details of the origin and meaning of townland names, arranged by parish for counties Antrim, Armagh, Derry, Down, Fermanagh and Tyrone, with some material relating to counties Cavan and Monaghan.

Typed extracts are also available for selected parishes in Northern Ireland and counties Cavan and Monaghan. Extracts from the memoirs in PRONI,

T/2383, include copies of topographical drawings which were originally prepared in connection with the projected publication of the OS Memoirs. The National Archives in Dublin hold officers' statistical reports for 38 parishes in Derry as well as papers relating to the publication of the Templemore Memoir. There are miscellaneous 'memoir-type' papers, including illustrations, relating to much of Ulster. There are also OS progress reports and OS correspondence. The National Library of Ireland holds the Larcom Papers. Also at the Ordnance Survey headquarters at Phoenix Park, are the field name books by John O'Donovan (on microfilm at QUB and PRONI), name sheets, memoranda and orthographical material. The Report on the Ordnance Memoir of Ireland (1843),which followed its demise, is available in the House of Commons Papers, HC 1844 (527) XXX. It was favourable but the government refused to budge on requests for its re-opening.

For those who wish to delve further into the history and workings of the Ordnance Survey, there are two indispensable books, by the acknowledged authority, Professor JH Andrews, formerly of Trinity College, Dublin. *A Paper Landscape: the Ordnance Survey in Nineteenth Century Ireland*, Oxford University Press, 1975, and *History in the Ordnance Survey Map: an introduction for Irish Readers*, the Ordnance Survey, Phoenix Park, Dublin, 1974. The former has over 300 pages with extensive footnotes, illustrations, tables and appendices appropriate for serious scholarship. The latter is no more than a 60-page booklet, but it gives the historian plenty of background information on pre-1922 OS maps, with 27 pages of illustrations of maps and plans and accompanying commentaries. The two provide a companion set which provides the complete guide to the Ordnance Survey in Ireland, which has split into two jurisdictions, since partition. The two Ordnance Surveys in Ireland came together in 1991 to produce *An Illustrated Record of The Ordnance Survey in Ireland* which is an excellent historical account with many fine illustrations.

EDUCATIONAL RECORDS

The most comprehensive archive of educational records relating to Ulster is in PRONI ref. ED/1. The national education system was founded in 1831, under the direction of the Chief Secretary, EG Stanley. National schools were built with the aid of the Commissioners of Education and local trustees. The aim was to replace the existing schools that had little relation to one another locally or nationally and standards varied greatly. The national system, it was hoped, would promote standardisation and mitigate religious exclusivity, allowing all children in an area to be jointly educated. However the schools often came under attack as 'godless' and clerical interference diluted their secular and integrated nature, even resulting in the establishment of rival schools in an area. In 1900 only 4 per cent of Protestant children and 1 per cent of Catholics attended a mixed religion school.

Some 2,500 schools in Ulster were set up between 1832 and 1870 and applications for grant aid yield much information about pupils and teachers (PRONI ref. E/D1). Inspectors' reports can be especially rewarding as they give revealing evidence about the state of education and the attitude of landlords, clergy and people to it in a locality. Also of interest are the registers which are the volumes summarising the education commissioners' dealings with particular schools. PRONI has a complete run of these from 1835 to the early 1850s, ref. ED/6/1. National school registers, from 1831, recording

Table 7: Appendix to the Second Report from the Commissioners of the Irish Education Inquiry 1826–7

Appendix no 22 – Parochial returns: County of Tyrone: Province of Ulster

Barony & parish	Diocese	Name of master	Religion of master/ mistress	Name of townland or place which school is held	Free or pay school and probable cost	Description of school
Drum-ragh	Derry	John McFarland	Protestant Established Church	Omagh Gaol	Free	The chapel of the gaol

Number of pupils in attendance on an average of three months preceding this return:

Protestants Established Church	Roman Catholics	Presbyterians	Others	M	F
4	41	5	–	50	–

Total Annual income of Master/Mistress	Societies, associations &tc with which the school is connected, whether assisted by local patronage, and in what manner stating such as are Parish Schools	Scriptures: whether or read or not in school
£181.13s	Kildare Place Society	AV

the pupil's age, religion, father's address and occupation are a good genealogical and local history source.

In PRONI there are some 1,500 registers for the Northern Ireland area and there is an alphabetical index for these in the *Guide to Educational Records*, which lists the very extensive and valuable holdings of this nature under the following headings: early education; national schools; private education; educationalists; Irish language education; tertiary education; pictorial; unions, societies and associations; copy-books, exercise books and programmes of work; school buildings; school inspection; model schools; agricultural schools and colleges; reformatory and industrial schools; nursery schools; government policy on education; local government policy; statistics on education; miscellaneous. The education records, particularly for the National Education Board for the whole of Ireland, are in the National Archives. The Ulster Folk and Transport Museum has the *Reports of the Commissioners for Education in Ireland 1834–1920*, in seven volumes on microfiche.

Table 7 is an indication of the kind of local information that educational records yield. It refers to the school in Omagh Gaol. It is not set out here in its original tabulation.

THE KILDARE PLACE SOCIETY COLLECTION
This is held in the Church of Ireland College of Education, Research Area, Upper Rathmines, Dublin 6, tel (01) 970033. Enquiries to the Honorary Keeper, appointment necessary and open normally during term-time. Guide, *Report on the records of the Society for Promoting the Education of the poor in Ireland* (Kildare Place Society), London Royal Commission on Historical Manuscripts, HMSO, 1982. The collection consists of administrative records of the society, general, committee, parliamentary, publishing and inspectors' correspondence; correspondence between the society and its schools. Originally state-founded and non-denominational, the Kildare Place Society was taken over by the Church of Ireland. There were accusations against its schools of proselytising. These records are useful to the local historian in the same way as those of the national schools.

RECORDS OF TOWNS IN THE 19th AND 20th CENTURIES

The English government originally envisaged plantation towns as self-governing. However, the plantation scheme was not properly resourced. Consequently, with the exception of Londonderry, which was already controlled by the London companies, the plantation towns soon fell under the control of local landlords, who governed them through manor courts. The landlords exercised political control by using corporations to elect MPs of their nomination. This was still largely the case in the early 19th century though there were now pressures for change. In 1800, Belfast became the first town to appoint people to conduct the day-to-day running of the town which now had a population of 20,000. In 1828 an act (9 Geo IV c.82) allowed leading rate-payers of any town to apply to the Lord Lieutenant to elect a body of town commissioners to look after paving, lighting and cleansing. This range of powers was increased by a further act, the Towns Improvement (Ireland) Act of 1854 (17 and 18 Vict c.103). The evolution of local government was completed with the Irish Local Government Act of 1898 which set up county, urban and district councils. The records relating to Town Commissioners and district councils is in PRONI, ref. prefix LA. These are fruitful wide-ranging records for the thorough study of a town. An excellent book on the subject is Virginia Crossman, *Local Government in Nineteenth Century Ireland* (Belfast, 1994). 'Sources For studying Ulster towns in the 19th and 20th centuries' has been published as an article in *Ulster Local Studies*, vol 18, no 1 (1996) by Dr WH Crawford formerly of the Federation for Ulster Local Studies. See also the recent publication *Sources for studying the town in Ireland* (Dublin, 1998), edited by W Nolan and A Simms.

CIVIL REGISTRATION

This was a further indication of the wider intervention of the state in society. While this is an area more appropriate to the genealogist, it should be realised that the local historian may have recourse to the General Register Office for information regarding the birth, death or marriage of his subject(s). In that case the following is useful. First, civil registration was only introduced in Ireland, around the middle of the last century. Prior to that, it was largely the prerogative of the churches. From 1 April 1845, all non-Roman Catholic marriages had to be recorded. From 1 January 1864, full registration by the state of all births, deaths and marriages began.

Since partition, these records for the 26 counties, have been held in the General Register Office/Oifig An Ard-Chlaraitheora, Joyce House, 8–11 Lombard Street East, Dublin 2, tel (01) 711000. Enquiries to Ard-Chlaraitheoir Cunta. Opening times 9.30am–12.30pm, 2.15pm–4.30pm, Mon–Fri. Photocopying available. Guide, Oifig An Ard-Chlaraitheora, list of records. The General Register Office for Northern Ireland performs roughly the same function. It is at Oxford House, 49–55 Chichester Street, Belfast BT1 4HL, tel (01232) 235211. Enquiries to the Deputy Registrar General. Opening times 9.30am–3.30pm, photocopying, photography and microfilming. Guides and information leaflets are available. See Catherine Blumson's extremely useful pamphlet on civil registration, published by the Ulster Historical Foundation (Belfast, 1996).

POLICE AND MAGISTRATES' RECORDS

Such records are increasingly being used by historians. Essentially they are reports to higher-ups by those with responsibility for the security in a particular area. While many are concerned with crime and disorder, and local historians are concerned with these, the records also give us information on many other aspects of life, for example the state of agriculture. The National Archives in Dublin have records going from the late 18th century to the early 1900s. For the period after that, the police records are in the Public Record Office in Kew in the Colonial Office archives (CO), and presumably out of reach to all but the most dedicated local historian. These reports were confidential and therefore we can assume that they were written with a view to accuracy and impartiality. There is some interesting information in Brian Griffin's *The Bulkies: Belfast Police in the 19th century* (Dublin, 1997).

The State of the Country Papers 1796–1820, vol 2 1821–1831

These contain the reports of generals and officers-in-command of districts and brigade majors of yeomanry. An example, contained in carton 431, ref. no 2298, is a report from Colonel T Pearson, enclosing a letter from Major Smith, Royal Welch Fusiliers, Greencastle, of a notice having been posted on the church door near Moville warning the people not to pay tithes and of a tithe proctor having received a threatening notice. (25 December 1821). In the succeeding period until the establishment of the police, the reports are filed as 'outrage reports'.

The example gives extracts from the confidential report to the RIC Inspector General for August 1894 by Owen R Slack, Divisional Commissioner for the Northern Division, which covered Ulster and Louth, with headquarters in Dundalk. It shows some of the scope of such reports which began in 1893. This was a period of evictions, boycott and retaliation, in which police had responsibility for protecting the legal occupiers. 'Protection is unchanged since my last report save that in Cootehill district, Co Cavan, a temporary Protection Post has been formed while crops are being saved on an evicted farm the property of Captain Quinn'. There were 62 'outrages' reported for August as opposed to 65 in July. One such gets into the report.

> In Raphoe District, Co.Donegal, between 1 and 2 a.m. on 28th August 7 men, 6 with blackened faces, assembled at William Tinney's house and fired shots. Tinney identified the man who was undisguised, and he has been arrested, The prisoner alleges that he has a claim to Tinney's holding which is the motive for the crime.

The report lists evictions on individual estates throughout the division.

There is an account of a meeting of labourers at Stewartstown, Co Tyrone protesting the failure of the local Boards of Guardians to build labourers' cottages. A large meeting of farmers in Ballymoney, Co Antrim, to discuss the proceedings of the recent Committee on the Irish Land Acts, is noted. There are accounts of political meetings such as as those in Drogheda, Dundalk, Newry and Omagh, addressed by O'Donovan Rossa, whose '. . . visits to the division have been decidedly a failure'.

Each monthly report includes an agricultural section which states in the following case,

> The prospects for farmers during the present harvest are so far most encouraging. It was feared that the excessive rain during part of the summer would have done great injury to the crops, but the fine weather which has followed has worked wonders, and all crops are now most promising. Potatoes in some places have been reported as slightly blighted, but nothing of any importance has appeared. The price of cattle is also good.

This shows the importance of agricultural well-being to the maintenance of law and order. Each monthly report has appended a form 64 which is a return by county of unlet evicted farms.

Resident magistrates (RM)
RMs also were required to submit reports to the Chief Secretary's Office. The following extract is from the 1890 reports of RMs Mr Hamilton (Donegal), Mr Beresford (Rathmullen) and Mr Bourke (Dunfanaghy). They are in the National Archives under the Chief Secretary's Office Registered Papers (CSORP/1890/17253)

> Owing to the general failure of the potato crop in the congested portions of Donegal District, mainly along the sea shore from Killybegs to Kilcar, Teelin, Glencolumbkill, Malinmore and Dowris, there will be very serious distress during the coming winter unless some measures of relief are adopted . . . In the better parts of Rathmullen District where the land is sound the potato crop is fair, and there is not much disease, but in the poorer parts, where the land is wet and boggy, the crop is inferior-size small-quality wet . . . Mr Hamilton reports that the employment for men during the winter is practically nil. In that season the women, by sprigging and knitting are the principal bread winners . . . The extension of the railway to Killybegs promises to give employment in a large tract where the people are comparatively well-off, but will not materially benefit such places as Kilcar &c'.

5

THE LAND QUESTION IN THE NINETEENTH CENTURY

As a result of the wars, plantations and penal laws of the 16th, 17th and 18th centuries, only about 4 per cent of the land was in Roman Catholic hands, by the early 19th century, although they constituted more than 70 per cent of the population. The vast bulk of landowners were of the Anglo-Irish Ascendancy class. The majority of the population in the south was therefore made up of catholic tenant farmers. The situation in Ulster was different to the extent that Protestant tenant farmers constituted a large part of the population. Nevertheless tenants of all religious persuasions had no real ownership or control over the land on which they lived and worked. In this lay the roots of a struggle for the land, between landlord and tenant, which was to last for the whole of the 19th century. It would only reach a solution with the land purchase acts, notably the Wyndham Act of 1903, which resulted in the break up of the landed estates and the conversion of tenants into proprietors. For the local historian, this turbulent era has generated a wealth of public and private records, arising out of the conflict and attempts by government to deal with it. Estate records in the National Archives and the National Library of Ireland are listed in Richard Hayes *Manuscript Sources for the Study of Irish Civilisation*, under landlord's name and by county. Access can be difficult particularly as many of these records in the National Library are not catalogued at all.

TITHE APPLOTMENT BOOKS 1824–38

A question, related in many ways to the land question proper, was that of tithes. Tithes to clergy of the established church were paid by all non-exempt inhabitants of the parish, regardless of denomination. Naturally this was a source of great discontent to those not members of the Church of Ireland.

Tithes had usually been paid in kind in the rural areas. From 1823, under the first Tithe Composition Act, the payment of tithes had to be made in cash. A commissioner was appointed, by the government, to make a survey of all the titheable land, in each parish, to determine how much was payable by each land-holder. This was not a comprehensive survey. As the tithe was based on roughly one tenth of a person's wealth, their relative status can be gauged from their contributions.

The books were done on a parish basis, though not all were done uniformly. While they all consisted of townland name, landholder's name, area of land and tithes payable, some also included the name of the primary landlord and an assessment of the economic productivity of the land, differentiating between arable, pasture and non-productive land. The tax was based on average prices of wheat and oats, over the seven-year period prior to 1823, and levied according to the quality of the land.

This had been a period of prosperity and valuation was higher than would normally have been the case. The resentment against tithes continued unabated until political pressure finally led to significant changes in the tithe laws and the abandonment of the survey in 1838. Tithes were not abolished as such, in the Tithe Rent Charge Act of that year. Rather they were mitigated into a payment to the landlord as part of the rent. He supposedly would be more likely to pay it to the established church. Nevertheless, payment of tithes in any form remained a bone of contention. After the disestablishment of the Church of Ireland payment, from 1871, was made to the Commissioners of Church Temporalities and, from 1881, to the Irish Land Commission. So land taxation still affected the farming community, even though the recipient changed.

Tithe applotment books represent the first major countrywide list and valuation of land occupiers and the most comprehensive information on the quality of land since the surveys of the 17th century. They are in effect a census of agricultural holdings in the years prior to the Great Famine and the consequent tide of emigration. They are useful as the only early records available for parishes where registers did not begin until 1850. They can also provide evidence for land being passed on from father to son between the Tithe Survey and Griffith's Valuation. *The Guide to Tithe Records* in PRONI, lists the tithe books for all but 31 of the 271 parishes that now constitute Northern Ireland. It lists by townland, parish, county, and date and gives the book reference. PRONI maintains an incomplete set of index cards giving the names of all those mentioned in the tithe applotment books, approximately 1 million cards. These are held in the library room, which is open to the public.

As well, the PRONI tithe records on microfilm MIC/442, cover almost all the parishes of Cavan, Donegal and Monaghan. The guide mentions in that case only those townlands which straddle the border. One problem for researchers is that local place-names do not always concur with those of the later Ordnance Survey. The PRONI reference number for tithe records is FIN 5A. The tithe books are available, in photostat, in the National Archives and on microfilm in the National Library, where surnames have been roughly indexed in the Index of Surnames. The Householders Index, produced by the National Library of Ireland, lists the occurrences of surnames in the Tithe Composition Books and the Griffith Valuation for all the counties of Ireland. These may be found in most libraries and repositories.

THE DEVON COMMISSION 1843

The population of rural Ireland had reached its peak, by the 1840s. The consequences of a combination of overcrowding and wasteful agricultural practices, led many to predict a disaster in the offing, rightly as it turned out. In 1843, the government appointed a Royal Commission, chaired by the Earl of Devon, 'to inquire into the law and practice with regard to the occupation of land in Ireland' (Her Majesty's Commission of Inquiry into the State of the

TO BE SOLD BY
AUCTION

In the Matter of	At *DENVIR's Hotel, in Downpatrick*
THOMAS M'HENRY,	on *Wednesday the 21st day of*
an *Insolvent.*	*September instant, at noon*:

THE Insolvents interest in that Farm in *Carstown*, in the County of Down, containing **34** Acres or thereabouts ; held by Lease under the Heirs of the late JOHN POTTER, Esq., for a term of Three Lives, Renewable for EVER ; subject to the Yearly Rent of £29 12s. 0d. *late Irish Currency*, and a Sum of £3 of the same Currency as a *Renewal fine.*

The Lands are situate about **2** miles from *Portaferry*, and will be Sold in One or several lots as Purchasers may incline.

WILLIAM M'CLEERY, Jun.
ASSIGNEE.

Portaferry, 10th September, 1836.

JAMES REILLY, PRINTER, DOWNPATRICK.

Notice of an auction in Co Down, 1836. (Linen Hall Library)

Law and Practice in Respect to the Occupation of Land in Ireland: Report Evidence and Appendices, in HCP, 1845, xix–xxii). The commission toured the whole country taking evidence, mainly from the landlord class and the clergy. Despite the narrow social base of their survey, they managed to collate three huge volumes of evidence which were later summarised in two volumes.

They reported on the land, under a wide range of headings, including ownership, occupation, valuation, subdivision, rent, absenteeism and middlemen. In the process, they unearthed a sorry picture of the conditions of the teeming, poverty stricken, rural masses. As well as the written reports, the commission produced many maps and statistical data to support their evidence. They were concerned also to report what improvements might be made, such as the utilisation of waste lands. Devon identifed some 3,775,000 'improvable' acres, a consequence of which was the 1847 Land Improvement Act, which allocated £3,000,000 to improving landlords. The Devon Commission has been included here rather than in the parliamentary papers section (see pp 31–3) because its reports on a county basis provide for local historians yet another contribution towards the picture of their locality.

THE ENCUMBERED ESTATES ACTS 1848 AND 1849

These were introduced as the result of the work of the Devon Commission. It wasn't only poor tenants who were affected by the Famine. Many landlords were bankrupted due to the inability of their tenants to pay rents as a result of the disaster that befell the country in the late 1840s. Add this to an already large total of existing bankrupted estates and it was clear that government action was necessary to restore much of rural Ireland to agricultural productivity. The action taken was the Encumbered Estates Act of July 1849. This provided for the compulsory sale of a debt-encumbered estate on the petition of either creditors or the landlord himself. It was hoped thus to transfer the land to more efficient and solvent owners.

A Landed Estates Court was established to effect the sale of estates, pay creditors and transfer title to the new owner. Over the next 30 years, some 5 million acres, amounting to a quarter of the total land area, were sold at comparatively knockdown prices. For the local historian, the bonus in the act is that the related sources provide detailed descriptions of the estates and rentals, prepared in order to attract or facilitate prospective purchasers. There are many maps of holdings and drawings of estate houses. In PRONI, there are 83 bound volumes of printed Records of the Encumbered Estates Court 1849–1858, refs. D/1201 and MIC/80/2 (sales index). The National Archives has a set of Encumbered Estates Court and Landed Estates Court Rentals, 148 volumes with indexes, 1850–85. See also the *O'Brien Rentals*, auction documents printed for the courts of Encumbered Estates in Ireland, Landed Estates, and Chancery Division. Land Judges sets are held in the National Archives and National Library.

THE RETURN OF OWNERS OF LAND IN IRELAND 1873–6

This modern Domesday survey, which was done also in England and Wales, recorded the numbers and names of all owners of land of one acre and more. The Poor Law Unions were given the task of extracting information from landlords, which was sent to the Local Government Board. There it was arranged alphabetically and published in 1876 as a government paper entitled 'A Return of Owners of Land of One Acre and Upwards in the Several Counties, Counties of Cities, and Counties of Towns in Ireland'. This has been reprinted as *Return of Owners of Land in Ireland 1876* (Genealogical Publishing Co Inc, Baltimore, 1988). Named landowners with one or more acres amounted to 32,614, unnamed, with less than one acre, numbered 36,114. From it, UH Hussey De Burgh, compiled the *Landowners of Ireland 1878*. This is a list of landholders of 500 acres or £500 valuation

"The house had once been respectable but had fallen much into decay"

*William Steuart Trench, agent for the Marquess of Bath, visiting tenant leader Joe McKay near Carrickmacross, Co Monaghan, 1851 (*Realities of Irish Life, *W Steuart Trench, Longman, Green and Co, London, 1868)*

and upwards. It is an abstract from the official survey of 1876 of all landholders.

THE BESSBOROUGH COMMISSION 1880–1

The Bessborough Commission, which took its name from its chairman Frederick George Brabazon Ponsonby, Lord Bessborough, was set up to investigate the serious consequences of the failure of previous legislation to solve the land question. The weakness in particular of Gladstone's first land act can be seen in the name and scope of their report. Its official title was the Report of Her Majesty's Commissioners of Enquiry into the working of 'The Landlord and Tenant (Ireland) Act 1870 and the Acts Amending the Same'. The 1870 Act, which attempted to apply the 'Ulster Custom' to all of Ireland and also to introduce a measure of land purchase, had been too little too late as was obvious from the current tide of agrarian disorder.

The commissioners went around the country and took as much evidence as they could from the different regions. There was criticism that there was no direct tenant representation on the commission. Nevertheless, in 65 sittings they heard evidence from some 700 witnesses, including 500 tenants, 80 landowners, 70 agents, the rest being clergy and professionals. In Belfast, they examined 56 witnesses, in Derry they saw a further 65, before moving to Donegal. For local historians, the commission papers are excellent for the picture given in evidence from different sources about the condition of the people and the land and in particular landlord–tenant relations at the time. It is useful for drawing comparisons between the different counties in respect of the workings of land legislation.

The upshot of the Bessborough Report was the second more interventionist land bill, which passed into law in September 1881. This gave tenants, the 'three Fs', fair rent, fixity of tenure and freedom of sale. It also established a Land Court, which became the Irish Land Commission, to adjudicate on fair rents. Nevertheless, the land question remained unsolved until tenants became proprietors as a result of further land acts. The Land Commission could also advance to the tenant three-quarters of the money needed to buy their holding. This process of land purchase was accelerated by the Land Purchase Act of 1903, most often known as the Wyndham Act, after the then Chief Secretary.

THE IRISH LAND COMMISSION, RECORDS BRANCH

The work of the Land Commission produced the Land Registry Archive, in which there are some 6 million documents with 530,000 fair rent orders and agreements. These were arranged by county and filed in boxes and volumes.

The bulk of the archive relates to land purchase up to 1923. There are different classifications of documents in the archive. Administrative documents are good sources for agricultural, economic and social conditions. These are documents relating to sales of holdings. Schedules of tenancies show annual rents. Surveyors' reports give information on acreages of holdings, their boundaries and the number of holdings on each estate.

Commission inspectors' reports on estates included type and quality of land, turbary (peat cutting) rights, any mineral deposits and even the conditions of evicted tenants. The inspectors had to report on whether the tenant was a good proposition to extend a loan to in order to purchase his holding. These reports facilitate comparative studies of conditions from one estate to another. In addition, the registry contains sections on title deeds and testaments and wills. The Office of the Land Commission, Records Branch is at 24 Upper Merrion Street, Dublin 2, tel (01) 789211. Enquiries can be made to the Keeper of Records, by appointment only. Photocopying is available. A special survey was carried out by Mr Ned Keane in the 1970s. He examined some 9,343 estates and wrote a brief report on each. These are bound in numbered volumes, indexed and available in the National Library of Ireland. The Land Commission archive also holds the records of the Congested Districts Board and the 17th-century Church Temporalities Commission. Land Commission documents, relating to the six county area, passed to PRONI after partition.

LAND RECORDS IN THE PUBLIC RECORD OFFICE OF NORTHERN IRELAND

There is a vast collection of records of landed estates in the Public Record Office of Northern Ireland (PRONI), covering all six counties of Northern Ireland. There are land records for estates in the Republic, most notably in Co Monaghan for which a book on relevant sources in PRONI is being prepared. In 1923, the first Deputy Keeper, Dr DA Chart sent an appeal to prominent families to lodge their records in PRONI. The third Duke of Abercorn, Northern Ireland's first governor, was the first to respond. There followed the records of great estates such as those of the earls of Caledon, Erne and Gosford as well as the Londonderry, and Verner papers. More recent arrivals are the Brownlow (Lurgan) and earl of Antrim papers.

The collections of landed estates and holdings large and small have followed into the archives. *Letters of a Great Irish Landlord; A selection from the estate correspondence of the third Marquess of Downshire, 1809–45*, (1974) edited with an introduction by Dr WA Maguire, published by PRONI, is an excellent example of such papers and their efficacy for the historian. *The Guide to Landed Estate Records*, which is available on the shelves of the search

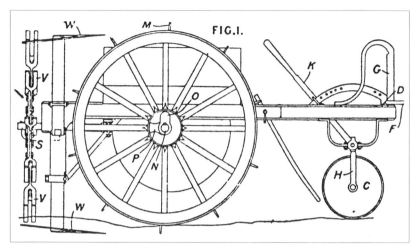

Drawing of a potato digger patented in 1852 by James Hanson of Doagh, Co Antrim.
(Ulster Folk and Transport Museum Archive)

room, is the easiest point of access. This is in two volumes, volume 1 covering Antrim, Armagh and Down and volume 2 Fermanagh, Londonderry and Tyrone. Each county is listed for maps, estate papers and land registry archives. The maps for each county are arranged chronologically and contain geographical and topographical maps of the county as well as for individual estates. Estate names are arranged alphabetically by estate/owner and include details of acreage and valuation, within each county. There is a description of the records and the relevant record numbers. The records for each estate are of course different and individual in many respects. However they generally consist of many of the documents that follow.

Rent rolls list tenants by townland; leases give the names of tenants and their families; rent ledgers show how much and when each tenant paid his rent. Wage books indicate those working on the estate, but not entered as tenants, such as labourers and servants. Muster rolls, militia and yeomanry lists are often included in estate papers. Note-books of land agents dealing with tenants and his correspondence with the landlord, particularly if he is an absentee, can yield valuable information. Letters between the landlord, his family and acquaintances, can complete the picture, at another level. There are often estate maps, usually on the scale of 6 inch to 1 mile, which plot tenants' holdings.

The Land Registry Archive in PRONI, arranged alphabetically by estate/owner within each county, has some 50,000 records relating to tenant purchase, arising from the various land acts, of the late 19th and early 20th centuries and the work of the Irish Land Commission (see pp 60–1). As most people in rural Ulster lived on landed estates until this century, these are almost essential records for the local historian, as they can give a picture of an area over a considerable period. *The Guide to Landed Estate Records* also includes lists of general maps of Ireland and Ulster, maps of Belfast and additional related land registry entries as well as an introduction to the land registry archive. *Co. Monaghan Sources in the Public Record Office* (Belfast, 1998) provides a guide to the archives of the landed estates of the county, most of which are in PRONI.

THE CONGESTED DISTRICTS BOARD, DONEGAL

As part of the Land Act of 1891, the Congested Districts Board (CBD) was set up to develop economically distressed counties of the west and south west of Ireland. It was an almost revolutionary measure of government intervention and can be viewed as part of its programme of 'coercion and conciliation' or 'killing Home Rule with kindness'. The board covered some 3.5 million acres, later extended by another 3 million, with 550,000 people, living on land so unproductive that they depended on a supplementary source of income, such as spinning, weaving, fishing, remittances from family in America or seasonal migration to Britain. Indeed, in evidence given before the Royal Commission on Local Taxation and later included in a report by the Irish Chief Secretary Arthur Balfour, the board secretary, WL Micks, painted the following vivid picture of poverty in these areas.

> In the Congested Districts there are two classes, namely the poor and the destitute. There are hardly any resident gentry; there are a few traders and officials; but nearly all the inhabitants are either poor or on the verge of poverty . . . the people are very helpful to one another – the poor mainly support the destitute.

Reduced rents or land purchase could make no significant inroads in this desperate situation. An area qualified for inclusion if the rateable value of its electoral division, when divided by the number of inhabitants, came to less than 30 shillings per individual. Despite efforts to have parts of counties Tyrone and Derry included, Donegal was the only Ulster county to fall within the ambit of the board. The east of the county and much of the area around Donegal town was rated too highly for inclusion. After 1909, the whole county was included, as part of a wider inclusiveness that put half the land of Ireland and a third of the population within the board's jurisdiction.

The board bought up largely unused estates for resettlement by people from unproductive land. By the time the board was wound up by the Free State government in 1923, it had purchased in all 1,104 estates totalling 2,587,597 acres. It encouraged the spread of scientific farming methods, such as improvement of bloodstock. It encouraged the fishing industry; indeed the letters CDB still overlook Killybegs harbour. It gave a great boost to the Donegal tweed industry and provided instruction in other rural crafts and industries.

For the local historian, the documents generated by the board provide an extremely valuable resource. This is especially so of inspectors' reports relating to each district, which were a detailed description of every conceivable aspect of life. They also contained recommendations for improvement schemes. WL Micks in his *History of the Congested Districts Boards* (Dublin, 1925) wrote,

> In my opinion these reports are of the greatest interest and value in showing what the condition of the inhabitants of the congested districts was at the time of the starting of the Congested Districts Board. Detailed and accurate information is given about the poorest districts in Ireland such as is not available in any other document; and these reports are doubtless of great historical value.

The inspectors' base-line or initial reports when compared with later reports, provide information as to the effectiveness of the work of the board. There is a base-line report, done by Micks in 1892 and included as an appendix in his book, running to 17 pages, on the county of Donegal – Union of Glenties, District of the Rosses, comprising the electoral districts of Annagry, Rutland, Dungloe, Maghery, Crovehy, Lettermacward and Doochary. This is an example of how valuable these reports are in creating a picture of Donegal from the turn of the century to partition. In that respect it can be compared with the Ordnance Survey Memoirs.

Written under the following headings:
Statistical table – district of the Rosses
Extent of the district
  1. Whether inland or maritime
  2. Average quantity of land cultivated in holdings at or under £4 valuation, under potatoes, oats, green crops and meadows
  3. Extent of moor or mountain grazing
  4. Whether land can be reclaimed or added to adjoining holdings
  5. Possibility of migration
  6. Method of cultivation &c.
  7. Information with regard to live stock and poultry
  8. Markets and fairs for sale of cattle and produce, and for the purchase of supplies
  9. Rail, steamer, boat, road, postal and telegraph facilities
 10. Employment for labourers in the district
 11. Migratory labour and earnings
 12. Weaving, spinning, knitting and sewing

13. Kelp and seaweed
14. Sale of turf-and nature and extent of bogs
15. Lobster fishing; number of men and boats employed
16. Sea fishing &c.
17. Number and class of boats employed in fishing or carrying turf or seaweed
18. Fish whether used at home or sold
19. Fish-curing
20. Piers and harbours
21. Salmon and fresh-water fisheries
22. Banks and loan funds
23. Mineral and other resources
24. Dealings – whether cash, credit or barter
25. Estimated cash receipts and expenditure of a family in ordinary circumstances. There follows an itemised cash account for a year of an average family in the Rosses; receipts total £43 0 0; payments total £42 15 5.
26. Estimated money value of the products of an average holding with other local advantages
27. Diet of people. Described in detail, for each meal, as almost entirely vegetable with little change or variety.
28. Clothing and bedding of the people
29. & 30. Character, disposition, dwellings, home-life, and customs of the people
31. Organised efforts for improvement of the district

William L Micks
Gweedore Hotel, Co Donegal,
27 May, 1892

The records of the CDB were transferred to the Land Commission in Dublin, where Ned Keane compiled a special edited volume of board records. The annual reports of the CDB, housed in the commission, are a very comprehensive source Also there are some 20 volumes of board minutes and proceedings. The *Royal Report on Congestion in Ireland* (HMSO, 1906) is another boon for in-depth research. There is a microfilm of the Congested Districts Inspectors' baseline reports for Donegal in the county library (see p 145).

6

MISCELLANEOUS RECORDS

WILLS

Wills are a very important source relating to the property-owning class. They give genealogical details of the testator and extended family. They can show how the fortunes of families have waxed or waned in a locality over the years. They are, particularly in the 19th century, indicators of the nature and extent of philanthropy. The National Archives is the main repository for wills in the Republic of Ireland. The National Library, the Genealogical Office, the Registry of Deeds and the Land Commission all have collections of wills. The Public Record Office of Northern Ireland (PRONI) holds all probated wills for Northern Ireland and some for the Republic, 1900–94, filed in a separate envelope for each testator. If a will was not made there may be letters of administration. There are Ulster probate registries at Belfast, Derry and Armagh.

There are bound annual indexes to the wills, covering the years 1858–1984, on the shelves of the PRONI reception waiting area. In general all wills prior to 1900 were destroyed in the 1922 PROI fire. However, each local registry had made a copy in ledgers before sending the originals to Dublin. These are available on microfilm, PRONI ref. MIC 15C. Also, bound, printed and manuscript indexes to pre-1858 wills and administrations are available in the public search room at PRONI. Because, prior to that year, wills were probated by diocesan bishops of the Established Church, the indexes relate to dioceses. The following are the northern dioceses:

• Armagh (Co Armagh, east Co Tyrone and south Co Londonderry).
• Clogher (Co Monaghan, south Co Tyrone, Co Fermanagh and parts of Co Louth).
• Connor (Co Antrim).
• Derry and Raphoe (central and north Co Londonderry and Co Donegal).
• Down (east Co Down).

- Dromore (west Co Down).
- Kilmore (Cavan, parts of Monaghan).

Although pre-1858 wills were destroyed in 1922, some copies are found in other records. There is a wills cards index, in the subject index section of the public search room in PRONI. Also, small family trees compiled from the pre-1858 prerogative wills are in the Burke Collection, PRONI ref. T/559, to which there is a typescript catalogue index. The Genealogical Office has the records of Sir William Beetham. These include his abstracts from Irish prerogative wills in 30 volumes.

PEDIGREES

PRONI has in its custody pedigrees for families from many different parts of Ireland, compiled by scholars, which are of enormous interest to genealogists and local historians. Most notable of these are extract pedigrees from wills proved in the Prerogative Court of Ireland between the 16th and 18th centuries compiled by or for Sir Bernard Burke, Ulster King of Arms. This collection of 42 large volumes of pedigree charts, are of great importance to all record searchers. Indexes to these volumes are available on the search room shelves (ref. T/559). Each volume has an index at the back and these are worth checking to ensure that you have seen all the entries for the family which are included in that particular volume. Pedigrees and genealogical papers relating to individual families can be located using the personal names index. A number of such papers have also been collected together under the single reference number D/3000. Researchers interested in the pedigrees of the leading landowning families in Ulster should consult the introductions in the respective calendars.

EMIGRATION RECORDS

The primary impact of emigration on the local community is change in the population. Emigrant letters are of interest to local historians in that the overseas writers often refer to life back home and the letters from home are often very good sources of information and news. An early anthology of emigrant letters is Patrick O'Farrell's *Letters from Irish Australia 1825–1929* (Sydney, 1984) which includes some 47 Ulster letters, taken from the collection of several hundred such letters, which PRONI have assembled and calendered. David Fitzpatrick's *Oceans of Consolation, Personal Accounts of Irish Migration to Australia* (Cork, 1994), is a more recent book and indeed a pathfinder in this type of work. In this book we are shown examples of how, as the author states,

In their search for consolation, writers in each country struggled to imagine life in the other. In trying to put that duality into words comprehensible at the other end, they minted fresh and distinctive images of Ireland as well as Australia, during a period of startling social change in both countries.

The problem for the local historian is how to locate letters relating to a particular locality. This is of course most difficult in the case of those sent out of the country. There were two great periods of emigration which affected Ulster. The first was mainly of Presbyterians to America. During the 18th century it is estimated that upwards of 250,000 'Ulster-Scots' left these shores as a response to religious persecution and economic harassment. They were to play a major role in the setting up of the United States and its subsequent history. The second great migration wave was occasioned by the Famine and its aftermath and affected mainly but not exclusively Roman Catholics. The influence of these Irish Americans continues to be important on both sides of the Atlantic. Also there are records for those many Ulster people who emigrated to Britain and the antipodes.

Some of the Ordnance Survey Memoirs, particularly of parishes in counties Antrim and Derry, contain lists of emigrants who left in the 1830s. PRONI and the Ulster-American Folk Park are the main centres of emigration records for Ulster. The most important type of record is the passenger list, which indicates who emigrated, from which port they left and their port of disembarkation. At no time, in the history of emigration, do we have comprehensive records of who left Ireland according to their place of residence. However, from the second half of the 19th century, detailed counts were made of those leaving Irish ports. The technique of 'cohort depletion' is a reasonable gauge of population change. This involves the noting of the number of people in a certain age group in an area in a census return for a particular year and returning to that cohort, 10 years later, to see the number surviving. In this respect, the number of those who died must also be known. The remaining number unaccounted for have migrated either internally or more likely externally. Of course this is a very inexact science and must be supplemented with whatever other records that are available.

The Emigration Database at the Ulster-American Folk Park

The Emigration Database is a very important resource, containing all sorts of information on emigration to North America, from the early 1700s to the 1900s. In the words of the museum publicity handout, it comprises passenger lists, emigrant letters, family papers and the diaries of emigrants, shipping advertisements, newspaper reports, deaths and marriages of former emigrants, births of children to emigrants, government reports and statistics

"ANCHOR" LINE.

Est. 1852.} AMERICAN MAIL STEAMSHIPS, {Est. 1852.

To New York, Boston, Philadelphia, Baltimore,
Portland, Halifax, and Quebec.

Alsatia,	3,500 Tons	Bolivia,	4,050 Tons	Devonia,	4,270 Tons
Anchoria,	4,168 Tons	Circassia,	4,271 Tons	Ethiopia,	4,004 Tons
Belgravia,	5,000 Tons	City of Rome,	8,415 Tons	Furnessia,	5,496 Tons

The above splendid Steamships, of Great Speed, and renowned for the Comfort
and Completeness of their Appointments, form

THE ONLY DIRECT COMMUNICATION BETWEEN

LONDONDERRY & NEW YORK,

SAILING WEEKLY,

AND TAKING PASSENGERS FOR

BOSTON, PHILADELPHIA,

And all places in UNITED STATES and CANADA.

Passengers are in good time to embark if in Londonderry by 11 a.m. on Sailing Day.
Luggage received on board from 10.0 a.m.

GREAT REDUCTION OF SALOON RATES.

FARES—First Class (Saloon) 9, 10, and 12 Guineas, according to accommodation.
Return Tickets, 16, 18, and 21 Guineas.

To NEW YORK, BOSTON, PHILADELPHIA, BALTIMORE, PORTLAND, or HALIFAX.

Second Class (Rooms of 2, 4, and 6 Berths, and including all Necessaries) and
Third Class (Steerage) at Lowest Rates.

Passengers Booked and Forwarded to all parts of the UNITED STATES and CANADA
by Shortest and Safest Routes, at Lowest Fares; also to AUSTRALIA, NEW ZEALAND,
CHINA, and JAPAN, at Through Rates, *via* San Francisco.
Low Rates to MANITOBA and the GREAT NORTH-WEST.
The Steamers are despatched from NEW YORK to LONDONDERRY Direct every
Saturday.
HOMEWARD CERTIFICATES from any part of the United States or Canada issued
at Lowest Rates.

The STEAMERS for NEW YORK LEAVE GLASGOW EVERY THURSDAY.

LIVERPOOL to NEW YORK (Via Queenstown), Regularly.

GLASGOW and LIVERPOOL to BOMBAY and CALCUTTA, Weekly—
Alternate Weeks to each Port.

LOW RATES to EGYPT and the HOLY LAND.

GLASGOW TO MEDITERRANEAN, Once every Ten Days.

Every information on application to appointed Agents in every Town in Ireland ; or
to HENDERSON BROTHERS, New York; Boston ; Chicago ; Marseilles ; 18, Leadenhall
Street, E.C., and 8, Regent Street, London, S.W. ; Bute Docks, Cardiff ; 17, Water Street,
Liverpool; Scott's Square, Queenstown ; 49, Union Street, Glasgow ; and

HENDERSON BROTHERS, Steamboat Buildings,

20, FOYLE STREET, DERRY.

General Shipping Agency for Australian Ports.

An advertisement from the Derry Almanac and directory, *1890. (Ulster Museum)* of Irish emigration to America and illustrated material showing ship types, ports, routes and maps, shipboard conditions and the cost of the voyage. There is online computer access to this database in the local history departments of the area library boards in Armagh, Ballymena, Ballynahinch, Belfast, Derry and Omagh. An appointment and probably a small admission fee will be necessary for this service.

Emigration records in PRONI

PRONI, in its home-coming series leaflets: 1 *Emigration to USA*, 2 *Emigration to Canada*, and 3 *Emigration to Australia* recommend the following emigration lists (emigration records) as being of particular interest to researchers:

USA

- T/711, passengers list from Warrenpoint and Newry to Philadelphia and New York, 1791–2.
- MIC/333/1, passenger lists – Philadelphia, 1800–82.
- MIC/333/2, passenger lists – Baltimore, 1890–92.
- MIC/333/3, passenger lists – Boston, 1871–91.
- MIC/333/4, passenger lists – New York, 1826–27, 1840–2 and 1850–2.
- T/1011, passengers from various origins arriving mainly in New York, 1802–14.
- T/3262, passenger lists from Belfast, Cork, Limerick, Derry, Newry, Sligo, Warrenpoint to USA, 1803–06.
- T/521/1, passenger lists from Ireland to America, 1804–06 (index available in *Deputy Keeper's Report 1929*).
- D/2892/1/1–14, passenger books of J & J Cooke, Shipping Agents. Sailings from Derry to Philadelphia, Quebec, St John's, New Brunswick, 1847–71 (see also MIC/13).

Some lists of emigrants are also available on the shelves of the public search room. These include: *The Famine Immigrants: Lists of Irish Immigrants Arriving at the Port of New York 1846–1851* (seven volumes, published in 1983) which contains data from the original ship manifest schedules, deposited in the National Immigration Archives in the Balch Institute in Philadelphia.

- Irish passenger lists 1847–1871, contains lists of passengers sailing from Derry to America on ships of the J & J Cooke and the McCorkell line.
- Passenger lists of vessels arriving at Boston 1820–21.
- Passenger lists of vessels arriving at New York, 1820–1821.
- Immigrants to New England 1700–1775, contains an alphabetical list compiled by Ethel Stanwood Bolton.

- Lists of emigrants to America 1635–1776, contains lists of passengers, including Irish emigrants who departed from English ports.

Canada

There is a vast amount of emigration material in PRONI illustrating the close relationship between Ulster and Canada for more than two centuries. These include shipping lists, school records, travelogues and regimental records. They are best accessed through the computerised subject index in the reception area (a print-out is available on the shelves of the public search room). Also of interest is the publication *Northern Ireland and Canada: A Guide to Northern Ireland Sources for the Study of Canadian History, c.1705–1992.*

The most important lists of passengers to Canada are as follows:

- D/2892/1/1–3, three volumes of passenger lists of J & J Cooke, Shipping Agents, February 1847–9, February 1850–August 1860, March 1858–July 1867, listing sailings from Derry to Quebec and St John's, New Brunswick, with details also for Philadelphia and New Orleans.
- T/3168/1, passenger list 11 May 1847, issued by the Chief Agent for Emigration, Quebec, giving details of Ulster emigrants.
- D/3000/82, comprises typed transcripts of notices in 19th-century Canadian newspapers regarding the whereabouts of Ulster immigrants.
- D/3000/104/1–10 contains newspaper inserts in Canada by passengers arriving from Ireland.
- T/768/1 is a list 1833–34 of emigrants from Coleraine, giving information on the names, religion, townlands of residence, destinations in Canada and date of departure of those involved.

Australia

Australian emigration did not get underway until the 1820s, after the disruption of the Napoleonic Wars. The government sent Ulster people to Australia either as transported convicts or on assisted schemes from workhouses. Some charities and religious bodies also played a part. Those emigrants who arranged their own travel to Australia were generally better off than those who travelled to North America, because of the higher costs involved in getting there. Thus a significant number set themselves up in business or bought their own land. Many Ulster people played a significant role in the shaping of Australia, eg Charles Gavan Duffy, from Monaghan, who became Premier of Victoria. The easiest way to locate the Australian records is to use the computerised subject index in the reception area (a print-out is available on the shelves of the public search room). The following records are of particular importance.

- MIC/468/1, indexes to male convicts transported to New South Wales, 1830–1842.
- MIC/468/1, indexes to male convicts transported to Western Australia, 1850–1868.
- T/3036, passenger list, 1840, Victoria, Australia.
- D/64819, register of the Girls' Friendly Society sponsored emigrants from various counties in Ireland, 1890–1921.
- MF/4, indexes to births, deaths and marriages in New South Wales, Australia, 1787–1899 index to names of assisted Irish emigrants to New South Wales, Australia, 1848–68, some arranged alphabetically by name of emigrant, with details of age, country of origin, name of ship and date of arrival, others arranged by ship, then by county and then alphabetically by name of emigrant, with details of place of origin, religion, names of parents and their address, and date of arrival.
- MF/3. For details of assisted emigration from the workhouses see the records of the boards of guardians (BG).

A very extensive bibliography of emigration records in Ireland and abroad and also of published works on emigration can be found in John Grenham, *Tracing Your Irish Ancestors*, (Dublin, 1992) pp 91–102.

MAPS

Irish cartography proper traces its origins to the 16th century when separate maps for Ireland began. John Speed's map of Ireland was the standard for the 17th century. Also important were the surveys of plantations and the work of Sir William Petty, particularly in connection with the Down Survey. In the 18th century, the consolidation of the great landed estates resulted in the proliferation of manuscript maps of estates and farms. An important name in the cartography of that period was John Rocque. Under an act of 1774, county authorities responsible for road improvements were required to provide printed maps for their respective counties. As a result of this, some 25 counties were mapped to the scale of between 1 or 2 inches to the Irish mile. In 1778, Taylor and Skinner published their *Maps of the Roads of Ireland*, which provides an excellent snapshot of the subject at a crucial period. Of course the science/art of map making in Ireland came of age in the 1820s with the commissioning of the Ordnance Survey (see pp 42–6).

The Alan Godfrey editions of old Ordnance Survey maps (catalogue available from 12 The Off Quay Building, Foundry Lane, Newcastle-upon-Tyne NE6 1LH), consist of maps, which are very useful for the local historian. They are presently available for areas in counties Antrim, Armagh, Derry, Down, Fermanagh, and Tyrone. Professor JH Andrews has produced two excellent works which show the value of maps to the historian: *History in the ordnance map: an introduction for Irish readers (1993)*. *Irish Maps*: No 18 in the Irish Heritage Series (1978). Professor RH Buchanan has a very useful article 'History in maps', Ulster Local Studies, vol 8, no 2, 1983. Kate McAllister, former local studies librarian, WELB, in her article 'Maps in local studies libraries' in *Ulster Local Studies*, vol 13, no 1, 1991 has provided a very comprehensive guide to how to access maps in Northern Ireland.

There are a considerable number of maps in libraries, museums and archives. For each repository consult the separate sections.

THE MAP LIBRARY, THE QUEEN'S UNIVERSITY OF BELFAST, SCHOOL OF GEOSCIENCES

Elmwood Avenue, Belfast. Tel (01232) 245133 ext 3346 or 3395
Opening hours: Mon, Tue, Wed 10.00am–12.00 noon; Wed, Thur, Fri 3.00pm–5.00pm

This is for the use of staff and students. However, the library is willing to provide help to local historians who ring or make appointments in advance. There are copies of ancient Irish maps, such as some Down Survey maps or Hamilton estate maps. Bound copies of the 6-inch Ordnance Survey of Ireland first edition and copies of revisions for Antrim and Down. Contact the librarian ext 3346 or ext 3395.

THE MAP LIBRARY AT TRINITY COLLEGE DUBLIN

Tel (01) 702 2087, fax (01) 671 9003; e-mail: pfrguson@library.tcd.ie
Opening hours: Oct–May, Tue 2.30pm–4.30pm; Wed 9.30am–1.00pm; Thur 2.30pm–4.30pm. Outside readers should apply for a reader's ticket at the enquiries desk in the Berkeley Library or write directly to the librarian. There is a library guide to the map library of which this is a synopsis.

Established in 1987, this is the largest collection in Ireland holding over half a million maps. The map library holds cartographic materials supplied on legal deposit or by donation. The collection consists of maps, published by the Ordnance Surveys of Ireland and Great Britain since 1801, as well as all kinds of specific modern maps, eg aerial views. It is one of the heritage departments of the library with rare older material as well as modern maps. However, manuscript maps are held in the manuscripts department of the old library. Many older maps are kept in the Department of Early Printed Books. Only a small proportion of the collection is as yet available to the public.

CHURCH RECORDS

In PRONI, the *Guide to Church Records* lists alphabetically, churches of all the main denominations with records deposited. Church records, for specific areas, can be traced through the guide. The main archives of the Church of Ireland are held in the Representative Church Body Library (see below). Nearly half of the pre-1870 Church of Ireland registers of births deaths and marriages were destroyed in the Four Courts fire of 1922. However, registers of around 200 parishes survived and have been copied and are held in PRONI. These marriage registers only go up to 1845, the date of civil registration. Presbyterian and Roman Catholic registers were not as systematic as those of the Church of Ireland and few have survived from before 1800. Presbyterian records in Ulster start in the early 19th century and Roman Catholic from around 1830.

Catholic baptismal records usually include the following information: date; child's name; father's name; mother's maiden name; name of godparents; residence of parents. Church of Ireland baptismal records, however, usually supply only the following: child's name; father's name; mother's christian name; name of the officiating clergyman. Church of Ireland clergymen, unlike their Catholic counterparts, also usually recorded burials under the categories of: name; age; and townland of the deceased. These burial registers often include families of different denominations. PRONI has copied the Presbyterian records and has microfilm copies of the Roman Catholic registers for Ulster, 1830–80. PRONI also has records for the Methodist Church, the Moravian Church and the Society of Friends (Quakers).

PRONI has the diocesan archives for all the Church of Ireland (DIO/) and Roman Catholic (DIO(RC)/) dioceses in Ulster. These are listed in calendars in the public search room. These diocesan records contain very interesting material on the life of the church and its people. Episcopal visitations are included in the Church of Ireland and Roman Catholic diocesan records, eg Armagh Visitation Records 1839 in PRONI ref. D10/4/29/1/14. Such records are not only concerned with the religious state of parishes, but also have a good deal to say on social and economic matters. There is a section on church records in Monaghan in *Co. Monaghan Sources in the Public Record Office of Northern Ireland* (Belfast, 1998).

Church of Ireland records

THE REPRESENTATIVE CHURCH BODY LIBRARY
Braemar Park, Churchtown, Dublin 14. Tel (01) 492 3979; fax (01) 492 4770 Opening hours: Mon–Fri 9.30am–1.00pm, 1.45pm–5.00pm except for public holidays and up to two weeks in summer. Admittance is free of charge to those who wish to read in the library during the normal opening hours. Application in advance is not required.

The library is the principal theological and reference library of the Church of Ireland and the major repository for the church's archives and manuscripts. The library seeks to acquire all published material by or relating to the church. Church of Ireland archives, mainly from the Republic of Ireland, which are no longer required in their original custody, are deposited in the library. Photography, microfilming and photocopying is at the discretion of the librarian and archivist.

DOWN AND CONNOR AND DROMORE CHURCH OF IRELAND DIOCESAN LIBRARY
Talbot Street, Belfast BT1 2LD
No telephone, enquiries to Hon Secretary. Opening hours and facilities by appointment.
Guide: JR Garstin 'Descriptive Catalogue of the Bishop Reeves Collection of Manuscripts' in *Down and Connor and Dromore Library Catalogue of Books*, Belfast 1899.

Major collections include the papers of Francis Hutchinson, Bishop of Down and Dromore 1720–39, correspondence of Lord John George Beresford, Archbishop of Armagh 1822–62, relating to the dioceses of Down and Connor. The manuscripts of the noted historian and antiquarian Bishop Reeves, Bishop of Down and Connor 1886–92, relate mainly to Irish Church history and antiquities. His work and that of his friend, the celebrated John O'Donovan are in many ways complementary and both have contributed greatly to the understanding of local history. There are many other documents and records of interest both to ecclesiastical and local historians, not least the records of Church of Ireland societies and organisations in the dioceses of Down, Connor and Dromore.

Church of Ireland vestry records
These have more than just religious import. The vestry is an assembly of parishioners meeting in and taking its name from the robing room of the clergy. In the past their business extended to much in the parish that could be classed as civil. Indeed much of the wide range of business dealt with could in fact be termed local government. For example, the vestry could raise funds for poor relief, parish constables, road repair, education and even recruiting for the army. The Select Vestry was an inner committee which levied taxes for church maintenance and payment of church officers. The money was raised from a parish cess, a local tax on householders and from the sale of pews. The applotment of the parish cess is contained in churchwardens' accounts or select vestry minutes. These are useful in building a picture of the local community. Indeed, after the penal era, membership of the General Vestry was open to all householders, though its officers had to be

members of the Established Church, which thus kept effective control. Vestry records are an excellent complement to other sources, particularly for cities and large towns. Many vestry minute books cover only the last 100–150 years. There are some exceptions, such as the Lurgan Parish of Shankill, whose minutes date back to 1672, PRONI ref. MIC/1E/33.

Roman Catholic records
Diocesan archives generally can be seen by appointment only and with reference required.

ARMAGH DIOCESAN ARCHIVES
Ara Coeli, Armagh BT61 7QY. Tel (01861) 522045
Enquiries to the diocesan secretary.
Major collections: correspondence and other papers of the Archbishops of Armagh, 1787–1927. Baptismal records (computerised only) of the diocese to 1900.

CLOGHER DIOCESAN ARCHIVES
Bishop's House Monaghan. Tel (047) 81019
Opening hours: 11.00am–1.00pm
Enquiries to archivist.

Guides, microfilm and catalogue in PRONI (see pp 94–7).
Major collections: papers of James Donnelly, Bishop of Clogher (1864–93). Baptismal and marriage records for parishes of the diocese to 1880.

DOWN AND CONNOR DIOCESAN ARCHIVES
73a Somerton Road, Belfast BT15 4DJ. Tel (01232) 773935
Postal enquiries only to the archivist. Photocopying facilities.

Major collections: Fr William McMullan correspondence 1803–09; Bishop Cornelius Denvir correspondence 1835–65; Archbishop William Crolly of Armagh correspondence 1835–49; Bishop Daniel Mageean correspondence 1929–62.

DROMORE DIOCESAN ARCHIVES
Bishop's House, Newry. Tel (01693) 62444
Enquiries to Bishop of Dromore. Access by special request only. Photocopying facilities.

Major collections: correspondence and papers of bishops, 1770–. Records of baptisms, marriages and deaths for each parish, 1926–. Other diocesan and parish papers.

KILMORE DIOCESAN ARCHIVES
Bishop's House, Cullies, Cavan, Co Cavan. Tel (049) 31496
Enquiries by post to the archivist, St Patrick's College, Cavan, by appointment or post.

Major collections: correspondence and papers of bishops including visitation books, deeds, plans, wills, photographs and press cuttings, 1836–. Archives of St Patrick's College, Cavan, including rolls, prize lists, deeds, plans and account book, 1869–.Correspondence and papers of priests of the diocese including the collections of Rev Philip O'Connor, Owen F Traynor and TP Cunningham.

RAPHOE DIOCESAN ARCHIVES
Cartlann Ratha-Bhath, Monastery Avenue, Letterkenny, Co Donegal. Tel (074) 36122/21208
Enquiries by post to archivist. Photocopying facilities.

Major collections: the episcopal archives, beginning with Bishop James McDevitt (1870–79). Papers of Bishops Daniel McGettigan, Michael Logue and Patrick O'Donnell have been acquired from the Armagh Diocesan Archives.

Presbyterian records

THE PRESBYTERIAN HISTORICAL SOCIETY
Room 218, Church House Fisherwick Place, Belfast BT1 6DW. Tel (01232) 323936 Opening times: Mon–Fri 10.00am–12.30pm; Wed also open 2.00pm–4.00pm

The society has many historical records, including the 1766 religious census for much of Ulster, the 1775 lists of Protestant householders for Antrim, Down and Donegal as well as the Presbyterian census returns, unique to the church, for the same year. There is an excellent history of Irish Presbyterianism, *A History of the Presbyterian Congregations in the Presbyterian Church in Ireland in Ireland 1610–1982*, Belfast 1982. This is a collection of short histories of local congregations.

Methodist records
A good source for a history of local Methodism in Ulster is undoubtedly

Evangelical Protestantism in Ulster Society, 1740–1890, by David Hempton and Myrtle Hill, 1992. This is very detailed and where it does not completely cover a particular area, its extensive bibliography and source list will point in the required direction. The book also deals with other aspects and branches of the evangelical movement in Ulster.

Religious Society of Friends (Quakers)

FRIENDS' MEETING HOUSE
Railway Street, Lisburn, no telephone. Enquiries to archives committee.

The Quakers have been assiduous keepers of records, since their arrival in Ireland in the 17th century. The records in Ulster begin in 1673 and include minutes of meetings, records of births, deaths and marriages, letters, wills and family papers as well as 'sufferings' records relating to discrimination and persecution.

Congregation histories
There are a vast number of histories of congregations of different denominations, usually produced on the occasion of an anniversary. In the best sense these are indeed the stuff of local history. They can usually only be obtained from the local congregation or branch library.

GRAVESTONE INSCRIPTIONS

These have been of most use to the genealogist. However they can be a useful tool for the local historian for whom the history of local families is an important adjunct. Many gravestone inscriptions, for counties Down and Antrim have been recorded in the *Gravestone Inscription Series*, edited by RS Clarke, published by the Ulster Historical Foundation. Others have been done by local history societies.

BUSINESS RECORDS

PRONI has one of the largest collections of business records in the British Isles, including the major Ulster industries of the past such as linen, shipbuilding and engineering, down to literally the corner shop. In the linen archive, which includes a printed catalogue, *The Ulster Textile Industry* (1978) more than 250 firms are represented. Linen records date back to the 18th century when it was mainly a domestic industry. The records cover the whole range of business activity from technical production and employment matters to marketing. Famous Ulster inventors such as Harry Ferguson, developer of the Ferguson tractor are included. The business records can be studied in tandem with related records of employers, trade unions, public utilities, solicitors, banks and government departments, to build up the local picture of trade and industry. The records of trade unions are complementary to these business records. PRONI has a large collection of the records of individual trade unions and trades councils.

DIRECTORIES, ALMANACS AND GAZETTEERS

Directories are an excellent source for the local historian. There are directories which cover the whole country, provincial directories, county directories and more local directories many of which did not survive more than one or two issues. Country-wide directories list all the cities, towns, and villages, starting first with a topographical and historical description of the area. They then list the nobility, gentry, members of parliament, town commissioners, Poor Law guardians, clergy, the professions, military officers and those involved in trade, commerce and industry. They normally excluded only the likes of small-holders, labourers and servants. Descriptions of public buildings such as court-houses, churches, schools and workhouses are included. Commercial directories are useful but were not officially sanctioned so their accuracy is not always beyond reproach. Some may only have included subscribers.

If possible, it is a good idea to compare different publishers' directories for the same area, if they came out around the same time. They can illustrate change in an area over the years, or facilitate comparative area studies. Country-wide, county specific and locality or town directories can be consulted in the local history sections of the county libraries or library headquarters. The best collection is held in the National Library, where most of the early directories have been transferred onto microfiche. PRONI keeps directories, on the shelves of the public search room. The following are the most important:

Thoms' Official Directory of Great Britain and Ireland has sections on counties, boroughs and municipal towns, with an alphabetical list of the nobility, gentry and traders. *Pigot's Commercial Directory of Ireland 1820* lists towns alphabetically, gives the names of the nobility, etc, and divides the traders of each town into their trade categories. A more comprehensive edition was issued in 1824. A successor to Pigot, *Slater's Directory of Ireland* 1846, expanded in 1856, 1870, 1881 and 1894, as *Slater's Royal National Commercial Directory of Ireland*, is arranged by province, giving trade lists for each town and village. It gives lists of nobility, gentry and clergy but excludes principal farmers. There are alphabetical lists of nobility etc for the main cities. It is also in the National Library, ref. NL Ir, 9141.

In what is now Northern Ireland, there were more localised directories, which are also kept in the PRONI public search room. *Martin's Belfast Directory*, 1839 and 1841–2 has an alphabetical list of gentry, merchants and traders and also a street-by-street listing of the principal streets. *Matier's Belfast Directory*, 1835–36 and c.1860 has the usual alphabetical list of gentry, merchants and traders living in and around Belfast. *Henderson's Belfast and Province of Ulster Directory*, 1843–4, 1846–7, 1849 and 1852, has a street-by-street listing and an alphabetical list of the 'principal inhabitants'. Its successor *Belfast and the Province of Ulster*, appearing various years from 1852 to 1992, gives a street-by-street listing for Belfast and the principal towns and villages of Ulster. *Thomas Bradshaw's General Directory of Newry, Armagh, Dungannon, Portadown, Tandragee, Lurgan, Waringstown, Banbridge, Warrenpoint, Rosstrevor* [sic], *Kilkeel and Rathfryland* [sic], which came out around 1819, includes an alphabetical list of traders but does not list local gentry.

In 1837, Samuel Lewis produced a two-volume *Topographical Dictionary of Ireland*, a companion to his earlier works on England, Scotland and Wales. The idea of such dictionaries was to provide a major reference work for popular consumption. This provides us with a very comprehensive survey of each county, ranging parishes within the county in alphabetical order. It gives detailed information on markets, housing, population, schools and churches for communities of any size. It is a good local source for pre-Famine Ireland of which it provides a veritable snapshot on the eve of disaster.

The following extract for Waringstown is a good example of the many comprehensive local histories contained in its pages.

Waringstown, a post-town, in the parish of Donaghcloney, union of Lurgan, barony of Lower Iveagh, County of Down, and province of Ulster, two and three-quarter miles (S.W.) from Lurgan, on the road to Banbridge; containing 825 inhabitants. The ancient name of this was Clanconnel, which was changed into that by which it is at present known by William Waring, who settled here in 1667 on lands purchased by him from the dragoons of Cromwell's army, who had received a grant of forfeited land in this quarter. The new proprietor immediately built a large and elegant mansion, which is still the family seat. In the war of 1688 he was driven out by the Irish army, who kept possession of the house as a military station till the arrival of Duke Schomberg, who remained here for two days on his way to the Boyne. Mr. Waring, who had escaped to the Isle of Man, was outlawed by the parliament of James II.

Samuel Waring, a descendant of the spirited individual to whom the place owes its existence and its name was the founder of its manufacturing prosperity in the reign of Queen Anne. Having acquired a knowledge of the processes for making diaper during his travels in Holland and Belgium, he introduced them into his own country; and the first piece of cloth of this description, made in Ireland, was the produce of his estate. He also, when abroad, procured drawings of the wheels and reels in Holland, and with his own hand made the first of the wheels and reels now in general use; before which, all the flax in the country had been spun by the rock and the spindle. The linen manufacture thus introduced and patronised became the staple of the district, and is now carried on to a very great extent in all its branches, there being scarcely a family in the town and neighbourhood which is not more or less employed in some department of it . . .

It goes on to list the petty sessions, police station, post office and church. It describes Waringstown House and mentions other gentlemen's seats and the houses of wealthy manufacturers. There is a brief topographical description of the district.

A similar publication, the *Parliamentary Gazetteer of Ireland 1846–9*, also by Lewis in three volumes, the *Gazetteer* was another form of directory or almanac, giving descriptions of Ireland in the period of the Famine. It was organised in terms of descriptions of counties, parishes and towns. The *Gazetteer* makes interesting comparison with the 1837 Lewis work. An extract for Cavan town on pages 384–6 shows the type of information on offer. It opens with the siting of the town.

A post and market town, the capital of the county of Cavan, and formerly a parliamentary borough, stands in the parish of Urney, barony of Upper Loughtee, co. Cavan, Ulster. It is situated on the mail-road from Dublin to Enniskillen, and on a tributary of the Annalee river, three and a half miles east of Lough Oughter, 25 south-south-east of Enniskillen, 25 north-north-west of Virginia, and 55 north-west by north of Dublin.

Environs – The environs of Cavan are nearly all undulated with swell, tumulus and hill, very various in outline, generally verdant in dress, and decidedly picturesque in character and grouping . . . all the beautiful country, around the town, is so grievously maltreated by a barbarous system of agricultural economy as to have both its pleasantness marred, and its vigour seriously neutralized . . .

Interior of the Town – Cavan consists of a street 1000 yards in length . . . a street, 430 yards in length going off from the middle of the former . . . Neither of the principal thoroughfares is straight; and nearly the whole town, with the exception of the new street and public buildings, is of unpretending character, and thickly daubed and patched as well as considerably prolonged, with rows of mere cabins. Yet, though neither lighted, watched, nor aggregately well-edificed it presents little or none of the abject meanness which characterizes many towns of its size in the west and south.

THE ROYAL HOTEL,

GIANTS' CAUSEWAY,

FRANCIS KANE, Proprietor.

CHARGES strictly moderate, and every attention paid to the comfort of Tourists, Excursionists and Family Parties.

Cup of Tea and Bread and Butter,	...	...	6d.
Tea, Preserves, etc.,	...	... ...	9d.
Do., with Boiled Eggs,	...	... ...	1/-
Breakfasts and Luncheons,	...	... 1/-, 1/6 and 2/-	
Dinner, ...	...	1/6, 2/- and 2/6.	

Sitting Rooms and Sleeping Apartments. Bed Room for One person, 2/-. For Two occupying One Room, 3/-. Attendance not charged in the bill.

Posting in all its Branches at the Lowest Rates.

Only First-class Wines and Liquors kept in Stock.

"The Royal" is denied the privilege of having a Porter to represent it at the Tramway Terminus, but Cars attend all Trams on the public road. Please look out for them. Parties driven to the Hotel free of charge. Coast Conveyances in connection with Through Coach to Larne arrive and depart from this Hotel.

Advertisement from County Antrim, 100 years ago: a guide and directory 1888 *(Belfast, 1989) first published as The book of Antrim by George Henry Bassett (Dublin, 1888).*

It continues at some length to describe the public buildings, such as O'Reilly's Castle, churches, schools, military barracks, and (in great detail) the gaol and the nature of those incarcarated therein. There is a copious description of the workings of the Cavan Poor Law Union and all its sub-divisions and dispensary. There follows a short description of the trade, commerce and infrastructural links of the town. It discusses at length Cavan's municipal government past and present.

George Henry Bassett brought out County Guides and Directories for Antrim, Down and Armagh. Historical reprints of Bassett's Guides were published, by Friar's Bush Press, as *County Down 100 Years Ago, County Armagh 100 Years Ago and County Antrim 100 Years Ago*. Friar's Bush Press has also reprinted *Lowe's Fermanagh Directory and Household Almanac for 1880* as *County Fermanagh 100 Years Ago, a guide and directory 1880*. These are very comprehensive county guides which give the history and topography of every town and village and surrounding area. Bassett's volumes contain over 400 pages (Lowe's is over 200) and as well as the usual alphabetical lists there are commentaries about local newspapers, sports and leisure activities and commercial and manufacturing concerns. Even hotels of note are included, giving a boost to the early tourist trade. The Bassett guides are excellent sources for local histories of Ulster in the late 19th century.

NEWSPAPERS

Newspaper collections are listed in the separate section on libraries (see pp 120–47). As a source for local history they are better from the late 19th century, as a reflection the life of the ordinary people, the bulk of whom could now read due to the National Education System. This was also why proprietors, usually with a political motivation, set out to appeal more to the newly enfranchised masses. They of course reported on the minutiae of day-to-day life in the locality, from court reports to funeral attendances. Practically nothing of any significance went unreported, in the local papers of Ireland, and to that extent they were and are parochial in the best sense of the word. Local newspapers have come and gone, over the last two centuries, but many are remarkable for their longevity and the continuity of recording of a local area that they provide. At present there some 40 newspapers affiliated to the Provincial Newspapers Association of Ireland, in the Republic, whereas in Northern Ireland 35 belong to the Newspaper Society of the United Kingdom.

Newspaper holdings in Ireland are listed in a number of works, the chief of which are as follows. *Newsplan*, the report of Newsplan in Ireland, by James O'Toole, published jointly by the British Library and the National Library of Ireland, is a comprehensive listing to earliest times. The 1992 edi-

For Sale at *Chichester-Quay*,

THE Brig WILLIAM, burthen about 120 tons.——She was built at Newn ham, Gloucestershire, and is only four years old. For particulars apply to Robt. and Wm. Simms.

They have just arrived per said Vessel, a quantity of BARK and CYDER; the latter is of an excellent quality, and will be sold very cheap by the puncheon or barrel.

Belfast, 17th June, 1789.

THE Presbyterian Congregation of Killinshy, beg leave to inform an impartial publick, that the Meeting-house now building at Lisbane is not only unnecessary, as the old Meeting-house is abundantly capacious and sufficient to contain the parishioners of Killinshy, Tullynakill and Killmud, but may prove injurious to the dissenting interest. The publick are requested to be cautious with regard to contributing to the above-mentioned building. Done at our Meeting-house in Ballow, by the unanimous voice of the congregation, this 21st day of June, 1789.

Signed by the Seshon Clerk,
JAMES LOWRY.

THE Presbyterian Congregation of Lisban, beg leave to assure the Public, that they are under an indispensible necessity to build a Meeting-house, as they have not experienced the most useful and pastoral labours amongst them for several years past: They solemnly declare they are the most decided friends to the Protestant Dissenting Interest, as their chief view in erecting a new Meeting-house is to promote the true interests of genuine religion—they therefore trust, that an enlightened and impartial Public will look upon any illiberal caution given to contract their minds and shut their purses—with the contempt it merits.

Done at Lisban this 24th day of June, 1789.

Signed, by the unanimous consent of the Congregation, by   ALEXANDER JOHNSON.
Seshion Clerk.

Advertisements from The Belfast News Letter *June 1789, reproduced from* A Belfast Chronicle 1789: a compilation from the Belfast News Letter, *compiled and introduced by James McAllister (Belfast 1989).*

tion is currently being revised. *The Waterloo Directory of Irish Newspapers and Periodicals 1800–1900*, Phase II, by John S North, published by the University of Waterloo, Ontario, 1986, is a very useful reference work, also being revised. *Northern Ireland Newspapers 1737–1987*, a checklist with locations, was produced jointly in 1987 by the Library Association (Northern Ireland)/PRONI Working Party on Resources for Local Studies. All three can be consulted in library reference sections. A more recent innovation with great potential has been the indexing of local newspapers by the library services. The article by JRR Adams, 'The use of newspapers as a historical source' in *Ulster Local Studies*, vol 8, no 2, 1983, is a very good introduction for the local historian. See National Library Publications, *The Past From the Press and Newsplan*.

PERIODICALS AND JOURNALS

These are not as fruitful a source as local newspapers though they are not without value for the researcher. A very useful reference work is *A Catalogue of Pamphlets on Economic Subjects 1750–1900*, by RD Collison Black, published by Queen's University in 1969. However, the standard reference work, held in the major libraries, is *Periodical Sources for the History of Irish Civilisation*, nine volumes, with an index, 1970, by RJ Hayes, former Director of the National Library of Ireland. Many local history societies bring out very useful journals dedicated to their particular area.

PHOTOGRAPHS

An essential contribution to the study of a local area is the photograph. Photography has been around since about 1839 in the form of daguerreotypes, which were supplanted from about 1850 by the more efficient Fox Talbot process which enabled the making of multiple copies. At first, photography was the prerogative of the wealthy, but photographic studios proliferated in the latter part of the 19th century, giving it mass access. The posed studio portrait is not so important to the local historian as the outdoor views taken by the professionals, to supply the tourist trade. This has left us a legacy of thousands of historical views most of which are safely housed in collections in museums and libraries. This was made possible by the wet plate (collodian) glass negative process, invented in 1851 by Frederick Scott Archer, allied to the development of portable darkrooms. Wet plates were supplanted in the 1880s by the less complicated dry plate process used by the photographers whose work form the major collections.

In addition to the work of professionals the arrival of the 'box-brownie' and its successors has given us millions of amateur photographs.

Photographs have now been around long enough to enable a long-term study to be made, making graphic comparisons over the years. We can see changes in places, in fashion, even in the condition of people over the years. The past is visible in day-to-day situations or in special, even historic moments. As a visual medium, one picture can convey more than a thousand words. It is more accurate in some respects than either the written word or sketch-work. One caution is that old photographs must be accurately captioned and dated, otherwise they could be misleading.

The following are the collections of most interest to local historians in Ulster. In the Ulster Museum at Stranmillis there are two major collections, the Hogg and Welch. RJ Welch (1859–1936) was born in Strabane, the son of a photographer. He came to Belfast, where he worked from the 1880s to the 1930s. He was official photographer to Harland & Wolff and the Ropeworks. He covered a wide range of topics including archaeology, botany, ethnography and botany. He was a member of the Belfast Naturalists' Field Club and it was the club which donated his large collection of glass negatives to the museum. This has approximately 6,000 plate glass negatives of Irish subjects, topography, industry, rural craft, antiquities, geology and natural history. The collection is indexed in two volumes, the first volume on topography and history being of interest to the local historian. The catalogue is organised on a province-wide basis. The Ulster counties and Belfast are conveniently referenced W01 to W10. Each county and Belfast is sub-divided and these are indicated on an accompanying published local government map, with a written description of each photograph.

Alexander Robert Hogg (1870–1939) came from Tullywest, a townland between Saintfield and Ballynahinch. He set up his studio in Belfast in 1901 where he continued to work until his death. His particular forte was industry, transport and architecture. He was interested in topography, portraits and social conditions. In relation to the latter, he was engaged by social reformers to take pictures to highlight the conditions in the slum streets of Belfast. The collection in the Ulster Museum, consists of some 5,500 glass negatives, about 1,500 glass lantern slides and several hundred prints. The museum has his register of negatives. Hogg also played a part in putting together the Welch collection.

Other collections in the Ulster Museum include the Langham Collection (c.1865–c.1918) which comprises some 100 items relating to the manor and village of Tempo, Co Fermanagh, taken by Sir Charles Langham. The Bert Martin Collection (c.1950–c.1965) consists of around 200 items on topography and portraiture. The recently installed Topographical Collection contains about 2,000 items on topography and portraits, with a name index. There is also a miscellany of small collections mostly from the turn of the century.

The Ulster Folk and Transport Museum (UFTM) at Cultra, Co Down, houses the collection of photographs of William Alfred Green. Born in 1870 in Newry, he served his time as a photographer with Welch, before setting up on his own in 1910. He worked in Belfast and later in Antrim, till his death in 1958. He concentrated on rural life and transport, hence the appropriateness of the siting of his collection, which covers the years c.1914–c.1935, in the UFTM. He captured many country customs and practices of cottage industry which have since disappeared. He also took photographs of the industrial linen industry. There are about 4,000 items with subject and topographical indexes.

PRONI contains many thousands of photographs, listed in a photographic guide. There are two main collections of photographs. One, covering the north-west counties, is usually known as the Cooper Collection, though it is the work of two Strabane photographers, JW Burroughs and HFT Cooper, to whom he sold his business in 1913. The Cooper Collection, ref. D/1422, has over 200,000 negatives covering the period 1901–60.

The Allison Collection, ref. D/2886, is the work of the photographic business of the Allison family, originally from Bradford, who came to Ireland in 1881. The Allisons took over an existing studio in 1900 and this collection reflects their work in the city and county of Armagh over a period of 53 years. Mr Ernest Scott, their successor in business, handed over the many thousand negatives to PRONI in 1962. Also in PRONI, ref. T/3390, there is the collection of Hugh, fifth earl of Annesley, of Castlewellan, Co Down, which is a fine example of the great fashion among the upper class for developing their photographic skills. Not only are these of great local interest but they show that for an amateur the earl displayed great technical expertise.

The National Library of Ireland (NLI) in Dublin has several collections of Ulster interest. The most important of these is the Lawrence Collection. The Dublin photographic business of William Mervyn Lawrence (1840–1932) took many thousands of photos of every part of Ireland during its years of trading. In 1943, the National Library acquired the negatives on the closure of the business. Most of the photos of views were taken by Robert French (1841–1917). There are 40,000 Irish views in the collection, taken between c.1880 and 1914, arranged alphabetically by town or county, in a main series catalogue. The negatives can be viewed on microfilm in several centres, such as Central Library, and Stranmillis College, Belfast.

In 1990–91 the Federation of Local Studies and the Federation for Ulster Local Studies, in collaboration with NLI and Fuji, re-photographed 1,000 Lawrence views. The effect of this is to monitor change and continuity. The Lawrence Project, as it is called, is available in NLI and those for Ulster are in the Ulster Museum. The Stereoscopic Collection contains 3,000 nega-

Strabane County Hospital, Co Tyrone, c.1918, from the Cooper Collection. (PRONI Ref: D1422/17/6)

tives, taken between c.1860 and 1883, by a special process which takes two near identical photographs on the same negative. These are viewed in a stereoscope to create a three-dimensional effect. This collection is also indexed alphabetically by county and town.

Valentines, a firm mainly involved in the picture-postcard business, has contributed the Valentine Photographic Collection comprising some 3,000 negatives of Irish scenes (c.1903–1960). It is catalogued on cards arranged by county and by town. The Eason Photographic Collection, consisting of 4,090 negatives of Irish scenes (c.1900–1940) is also catalogued by county. These collections provide us with a comprehensive photographic record of Ireland in the late 19th and early 20th centuries. The Lawrence new series, stereoscopic, Eason and Valentine collections are not on microfilm and cannot be viewed, but prints can be purchased.

A more recent development has been aerial photography which literally gives a bird's-eye view of the locality. The Morgan Collection of 3,000 negatives (1954–7) came from the aerial camera of Captain Alexander Campbell Morgan DFC, trading as Aerophotos. Most of the photographs were commissioned by clients such as newspapers, industrialists, schools and religious orders. Morgan was killed, at the age of 38, when his plane crashed near Shannon in 1958. The collection, which covers most counties in Ireland, was acquired in 1991. There are also aerial photographs in PRONI and the Belfast Public Library has a collection of more recent photographic surveys including the aerial photography of Aerofilm Ltd, from 1950.

The National Museum of Ireland holds an extensive photographic archive, such as the Mason Collection (rural life, mainly from the 1920s and 1930s), the St Joseph Collection of Aerial Photographs (archaeology and landscape) and the Cashman Collection (political and current affairs, emphasis on 1916–23). Most holdings are accessible for consultation and also purchase.

The following is a list of the various other sources of photographic collections arranged by county.

Antrim

The Irish World Organisation's Ballycastle Museum has a small collection including some by Welch relating to north Antrim. The Central Library in Belfast has the Lawrence Collection on microfilm, Welch prints and other photographs relating to the city and district. Lisburn Museum has Lawrence, Welch, Green and Hogg photographs for the area. The Linen Hall Library in Belfast has a large collection of more recent photographs of the Shankill area by Buzz Logan.

The Environment and Heritage Service (Department of the Environment NI) in Hill Street, Belfast has three major collections. The Buildings

Collection has approximately 45,000 black and white photos and 15,000 slides. The Archaeological Collection contains about 30,000 black and white photos and 12,500 slides. The only index available for this is in *Archaeological Survey of County Down*, Belfast: HMSO, 1966. The McCutcheon Archive contains over 20,000 black and white prints and negatives relating mainly to buildings of industrial interest in the six counties of Northern Ireland and some to counties Monaghan and Donegal.

The Ordnance Survey of Northern Ireland in Stranmillis Road has a collection of approximately 75,000 aerial photographs of Northern Ireland dating from the 1960s. They are accessed by grid coordinates. The Queen's University of Belfast, Architecture Department, has a collection of negatives of listed buildings in Northern Ireland, photographed by Christopher Hill. These are duplicates of the originals held in the Environment and Heritage Service. The North Eastern Education and Library Board (NEELB) Library HQ in Ballymena has the Lawrence Collection on microfilm as well as prints for the area. It has various small collections some of which can be seen in its branches at Antrim and Coleraine in the Irish Room.

Armagh

Armagh County Museum has many prints relating to the city and county (see subject index). At the Southern Education and Library Board (SELB) Library HQ, in Armagh City, there are Lawrence microfilm and prints of the area.

Derry

In Derry City, the Western Education and Library Board (WELB) Central Library Irish and Local History Department has a collection of indexed photographs relating to the county (see Derry Central Library, pp 132–3). Magee College of the University of Ulster has an extensive collection of historic photographs of the north-west.

Down

Ballynahinch Library HQ of the South Eastern Education and Library Board (SEELB) has Lawrence and Welch prints for Co Down and south Antrim as well as the full Lawrence Collection on microfilm. They have photographs dating from the 1970s onwards and various other small collections. In Newry, the Museum and Arts Centre holds the Myles Gilligan Collection (1945–50) of about 60 topographical prints and negatives. It also has Lawrence prints, family and guidebook photographs relating to the area. The North Down Heritage Centre in Bangor has Green photographs of Bangor which were probably done for official guides as well as other local historic photographs. Down County Museum in Downpatrick has Lawrence and

Welch prints. Its Co Down Photographic Collection has a topographical index. It includes the work of Thomas Gribben of Loughinisland who was a farmer and photographer who recorded the political and cultural events in Loughinisland, Co Down, from the Home Rule Crisis 1912 to World War Two. Dan J McNeill was a photographer who recorded life, in and around Dundrum, Co Down, from the 1940s to the 1960s.

Fermanagh
Fermanagh County Museum has Lawrence and Welch prints and many small collections relating to the area, indexed by subject. The WELB Fermanagh Divisional Library, in Enniskillen, has Lawrence photographs and smaller collections relating to the county.

Tyrone
In the Omagh Library of the WELB (Tyrone Division), there is the Lawrence Collection on microfilm and prints relating to the area and some smaller collections dating back to the start of the century. They are arranged in topographical order with a subject and name index. The Irish World in Dungannon has a collection of photographs to supplement its genealogical and local history research. It provides subject, name and topographical indexes for its collection.

(For photographs in Cavan, Donegal and Monaghan, see pp 141–6. For further details, on photography, see the excellent article by Patricia Webb, 'Ulster in photographs: a guide to the collections' in *Ulster Local Studies*, vol 12, no 1, Summer 1990.)

Photographic books
This is one area in which the local historian is well-served by publishers. The many books based on the collections above have been best sellers also with the general readership. Publishers like Friar's Bush Press, Blackstaff and Appletree, among others have covered almost every individual area of Ulster in this respect. Also, such books have looked at topics or themes. This makes the job of the local historian easier. It is invidious to single out individual books and the relevant books on their own local area will already be known to each local historian. However, it is worth noting some works relating to the main collections. Many contain useful notes to those collections.

- Hickey, K (ed) *The light of other days: Irish life at the turn of the century in the photographs of Robert French*. London, 1973.
- Evans, E Estyn and Turner, Brian *Ireland's Eye: The photographs of Robert John Welch 1859–1936*. Belfast, 1977.
- Maguire, WA *Caught in time: the photographs of Alexander Hogg of Belfast 1870–1939*. Belfast, 1986.

• Walker, Brian M *Shadows on glass: a portfolio of early Ulster photography.* Belfast, 1976.

SOLICITORS' RECORDS

PRONI has in all more than 140 large Northern Ireland solicitors' collections. They can be found in the subject index under the heading 'Legal system: solicitors and attorneys'. The deposit of L'Estrange and Brett, Belfast is most important in the east of Northern Ireland, containing a large and wide-ranging array of records relating to linen manufacturers, distillers, chemical works, potato sales during the Famine, Belfast Improvement Schemes and the Belfast Philharmonic Society. The collection of Wilson and Simms, Strabane is of similar importance west of the Bann. They were Unionist election agents from 1885 to 1920, and the collection includes much political and election material for the north Tyrone constituency. The records of the firm of Carleton, Atkinson and Sloan, Portadown contain title deeds, legal papers, Irish Land Commission records, etc relating to the estates of the Wakefield and Richardson families at Moyallon and Gilford, Co Down and in the Lurgan and Portadown area. The Martin and Brett Collection from Monaghan contains the records of many of the landed families of the county.

Solicitors' collections, comprising title deeds, testamentary papers, inventories, valuations, as well as the firms' archives in the form of journals, letter books and accounts, are invaluable as a source to the local and business historian. They also provide numerous copies of destroyed Irish public records. They fall into two main types: (a) office administration; and (b) clients' papers. The latter are of principal interest to genealogists and the local historian as they include records of prominent landowning families which create a picture of a particular family or area. They can include titles, deeds, testamentary papers, leases maps and rentals. In order to find the records of a particular firm of solicitors in PRONI, see the subject index under the heading 'Legal system: solicitors and attorneys'.

ARCHITECTURE AND BUILDING RECORDS

The architectural heritage of Ulster is very much a topic for the local historian. The built environment is the most concrete evidence of the past. The Ulster Architectural Heritage Society is where those with an interest in the architectural heritage and its conservation have banded together. The society has a number of functions, one being the publication of works on historic buildings and areas. The other work of importance is the preservation of such buildings, especially those which may be endangered through neglect, redevelopment or inappropriate redesign. In this last respect, the society has a buildings at risk officer and a computer-based buildings at risk register.

The society, in association with the Monuments and Buildings Record, Environment and Heritage Service (DOENI), has published an excellent five-volume *Catalogue of Historic Buildings at Risk in Northern Ireland*, volume 1, Autumn 1993, volume 2, January 1995. This gives a photograph, location, Ordnance Survey map number, grid reference and status of building, eg listed. Each entry includes a written description with any additional references. The Ulster Architectural Heritage Society is at 185 Stranmillis Road, Belfast, BT9 5DU, tel (01232) 660809. Other bodies such as Belfast and Derry Civic Trusts carry on related work.

For those who wish to progress to a special study of buildings, a prerequisite is the periodical *The Irish Builder*, which began publication as *The Dublin Builder* in 1859, changing to its present title in 1867. It is a blend of contemporary architectural and antiquarian interests. It can be consulted in university libraries. The library of the Ulster Folk and Transport Museum (see pp 109–11) has *The Irish Builder* on microfiche, 18 reels, for 1859–1900. Recently, European Micropublishing Services, 10 Cornelstown Hill, Foxrock, Dublin 18, tel (01) 289 7912, have brought out *The Irish Builder* in a complete bound set of 654 microfiches.

TRAVELLERS' ACCOUNTS

A source of information on local history is visitors' descriptions. Tourists and others travelling around Ireland have left us with copious descriptions of the country at different periods. Obviously these narratives can be of different degrees of reliability depending on the writer. A useful book on these observers is T Heaney, *Tourists in Ireland 1800–1850; an annotated bibliography*, London, 1968. The following is only a sample of the most important travellers' accounts: Twiss, R *A Tour in Ireland*, 1775; Young, A *Tour in Ireland*, 2 vols, 1780; Wakefield, E *View of Ireland*, 1812; Inglis, HD *Journey Through Ireland*, 1834; Barrow, J *Tour around Ireland*, 1835. Thackery's *The Irish Sketch Book* (1842), who travelled in Ireland on Post Office business, is worth looking at.

Many libraries have listings of travellers' accounts.

7

ARCHIVES AND RECORD OFFICES

ARCHIVES AND RECORD OFFICES IN NORTHERN IRELAND

THE PUBLIC RECORD OFFICE OF NORTHERN IRELAND (PRONI)

66 Balmoral Avenue, Belfast BT9 6NY. Tel (01232) 251318; fax (01232) 255999; e-mail: proni@nics.gov.uk; Internet website address http://proni.nics.gov.uk/index.htm
To arrange group visits in advance, ask for ext 215 or 267.
Opening hours: Mon–Fri 9.15am to 4.45pm (8.45pm Thur). Last document order is at 4.15pm (8.15pm Thur).

The Public Record Office of Northern Ireland opened in March 1924. Its first job was to replace the records, relating to Northern Ireland that were lost in the 1922 Four Courts fire and through the partition of the country. PRONI was also to become the repository of all public records generated in the new Northern Ireland state. In addition, from the start, it sought records from other provenance, mainly from within Northern Ireland, such as estate papers, church archives, records of institutions, private individuals, business and solicitors' papers, all of which are invaluable to the historian.

There is an excellent *Guide to the Public Record Office of Northern Ireland* to facilitate access to the millions of documents of which there are 33 shelf miles. There are also many PRONI leaflets, describing different types of individual records, which have been very useful in compiling this book. Two series of these are *Your Family Tree* and *Local History*. There are ring-bound guides such as the *Guide to Church Records* (with the Ulster Historical Foundation). As of writing this, the *Guide to County Sources* has been

94

published for Fermanagh and Armagh, with Tyrone soon to follow and the other counties eventually. Also published is *Co. Monaghan Sources in the Public Record Office of Northern Ireland* (Belfast, 1998), mainly on the landed estates. Other PRONI guides include the *Guide to Tithe Records*, the *Guide to Sources for Women's History*, the *Guide to Landed Estate Records* in two volumes, the *Guide to the Records of the London Companies*, the *Guide to Educational Records* and even the *Guide to Cabinet Committees* and *Guide to Cabinet Conclusions 1921–43*. These last guides reflect the essentially local nature of Northern Ireland politics in its early stages and can be of interest to the local historian. The Annual Reports of the Deputy Keepers of Records are useful in providing an overview of its work and in noting recent accessions or acquisitions. A guide to local history sources in PRONI is being prepared.

The *Guide to the Public Record Office of Northern Ireland* should be read, in advance of the first visit if possible, to cut down on the often limited time we have for actually perusing the records. The following is a synopsis of this. The public search room contains two extensive card indexes; one for personal names and one for place names (at present being computerised). The Householders Index, produced by the National Library of Ireland, lists the occurrences of surnames in the Tithe Applotment Books and the Griffith Valuation for all the counties of Ireland. There is a copy on the shelves of the search room in PRONI. The *Alphabetical Index to the Townlands and Towns, Parishes and Baronies of Ireland* is also available on the search room shelves at PRONI, NLI, etc and is the easiest way to trace the place you are looking for. There is also a computerised print-out and a guide for the subject index. The public search room shelves contain bound typescript catalogues of the listed collections of documents in the office. Each collection of documents in PRONI is given a collection number and, where possible, each document is sub-numbered with a brief description. There is also an extensive selection of directories and almanacs in the public search room (see pp 79–83).

The Groves Manuscripts

Also of interest are the Groves Manuscripts which contain a great deal of valuable material for genealogists. Tenison Groves, a Belfast genealogist and record searcher for more than 40 years, compiled a collection of many thousands of transcripts, abstracts, notes, etc, which he made from records in the Public Record Office in Dublin before its partial destruction in 1922. That part of the collection which related to Northern Ireland was purchased by PRONI in 1939. The items, numbering over 9,000 includes 17th century muster rolls, militia lists and family pedigrees and is an invaluable source for genealogists. The genealogical material in the Groves Collection has been arranged roughly by surname starting with the same letter. The arrangement under each letter is not strictly alphabetical and material on one name can

The Market-Town

OF

LURGAN

TO WIT.

REMOVAL OF NUISANCES.

11 *and* 12 *Victoria, Cap.* 123.

THE TOWN COMMISSIONERS hereby give Notice, that it is their intention to Prosecute all Owners or Occupiers of Dwelling Houses or other Buildings, within the limits of the TOWN OF LURGAN, which are in an Unwholesome or Filthy condition, unless these Houses and Buildings be forthwith Cleansed and Whitewashed, both outside and in.

And they further require that all Manure Heaps and accumulations of Offensive or Noxious Matter be forthwith removed from all the Streets, Lanes, Gateways, and Passages of the said Town.

They wish to impress upon the Inhabitants the necessity there is, for the sake of their own healths, in having the utmost cleanliness preserved in all the Public Thoroughfares, and their determination of putting the powers of the Law into immediate and active force against any infringement of the Cleansing Regulations of the Town. Every Inhabitant is required to have the Footpath in front of his or her House, swept before 10 o'clock each Morning, (Sundays excepted) under a penalty not exceeding Two Shillings for each offence.

Furthermore, the Commissioners desire to intimate, that they have given HENRY M'SHANE, their Inspector, and WILLIAM DAVIS, the Town Scavenger, strict injunctions to Prosecute all parties neglecting to conform to the above Regulations.

SIGNED,

HENRY GREER,

Clerk to the Commissioners.

Lurgan, 18th November, 1849.

[EVANS. Printer, opposite Northern Bank, Lurgan

'00 Copies

Printed notice concerning the 'removal of nuisances' from the market town of Lurgan, Co Armagh, 1849. (Public Record Office of Northern Ireland: PRONI ref. LA51/50D/2) appear in several volumes. The Groves Manuscripts have been given the PRONI reference number T/808 and the catalogue, which features typescript extracts from these records, is available on the shelves of the public search room.

Sectional lists
These give a brief summary of certain categories of documents. They give references which direct readers to the typescript catalogues. There are sectional lists for the following: textile industry records; landed estates records; church records; maps, plans and surveys (pre-1830); photographs; records of the London Companies; Irish post office records; encumbered estates records; records relating to Rathlin Island; sources for the study of local history in Northern Ireland.

The records of the county, district and urban councils, town commissioners and Grand Juries dating mainly from the 19th but also from the 18th centuries are available. There is also material relating to manor courts. Indeed many of these records predate the 19th century, so the researcher can get a picture of the early evolution of local government. Sports records of all kinds are available in PRONI. The following records are simply listed here, though many are dealt with in detail in the records section of this book (pp 9–93), giving the relevant PRONI references. These include: Grand Jury records; town commissioners' records; tithe applotment records; valuation records; maps, plans and surveys; Poor Law records; school records; church records; landed estates records; business records; solicitors' records; records of private individuals; photographic records.

PRONI on the Internet (http://proni.nics.gov.uk/index.htm)
With its own website, which at present sustains the second highest number of hits in Northern Ireland, PRONI is moving to a position where online browsing of much of its archives will be available to people worldwide at home or their place of study or work 24 hours a day. This will be a boon to the local historian for whom a trip to PRONI may be time-consuming.

As well as being the Public Record Office for the whole of Northern Ireland, PRONI also acts as the records office for each of the six counties and fulfils the function of the manuscripts department of a national library. Thus Northern Ireland's records are uniquely concentrated and the researcher has the benefit of one-stop access to archives from the best possible variety of sources, which in other jurisdictions, are scattered among different institutions. For Ulster local historians, particularly those living in the six counties of Northern Ireland, this is without doubt the main archive of public and private sources. It is also the major source of genealogical information for those of Ulster ancestry.

THE MONUMENTS AND BUILDINGS RECORD, ENVIRONMENT AND HERITAGE SERVICE (DOENI)

5–33 Hill Street, Belfast BT1 2LA. Tel (01232) 235000; fax (01232) 310288
Opening hours: 9.30am–4.30pm (closed 1.00pm to 2.00pm for lunch)

The Monuments and Buildings Record (MBR) was officially opened to the public on 27 October 1992. It is housed in the Environment and Heritage Service premises, a listed building formerly the property of Old Bushmills Distillers, in Hill Street, Belfast. It is open to the public but as a relatively new facility it is still very much at the development stage. The MBR is also used by the staff of the Environment and Heritage Service as a tool in their work. The records in MBR are varied in their origins and functions. The main one is the Northern Ireland Sites and Monuments Record (SMR), established in the 1970s, which contains information on some 12,800 archaeological sites. The SMR is a map-based database in list and map form for the protection of the sites. It is distributed to government departments which interact with landowners and the general public. These records also contain site descriptions, card indices, management files, photographs, transparencies and drawings. SMR includes the archives and artifacts of archaeological excavations, most of them done by MBR. MBR is aiming for total computerisation. There is a statutory list of some 8,000 listed buildings. The Buildings Record, begun in the 1950s, has details of listed and non-listed buildings, many of which were donated from architectural and other sources.

The Historic Gardens Record
This was compiled in the Institute of Irish Studies, by Belinda Jupp, and deposited at the MBR by the NI Heritage Gardens Committee. It contains details of over 600 historic gardens. It is a facility which is of interest to the local historian, as well as the historian of country houses and gardens. The list is arranged on a county basis and within the county, gardens are listed alphabetically. Not all are stately home gardens. The term heritage garden is explained in the accompanying glossary, which also includes a potted history of gardens in Ireland.

The Industrial Heritage Record
This contains both the Industrial Archaeology Record for the whole of Ulster and the Greater Belfast Industrial Archaeology Survey. Present also is the extremely important McCutcheon Archive, which is on loan from PRONI. This is a comprehensive survey carried out in the 1960s by WA McCutcheon, formerly director of the Ulster Museum, of monuments and features relating to the industrial and commercial life of Ulster in the pre-

A drawing of the carved representation of the continent of Europe from the facade of McCausland's seed warehouse, Victoria Street, Belfast. This 19th-century building is now a hotel. (Environment and Heritage Service (DOENI))

ceding three centuries. It has over 20,000 photographs of the six counties of Northern Ireland, as well as some relating to canals and railways in Monaghan and Donegal. Many of these studies were made prior to their subjects being removed from the landscape. An example of such is the canal and railway networks and their accompanying building and engineering structures. The archive also includes copies of the huge number of government documents, company papers, plans and notebooks, down to items such as lock-keepers' records that were used in the prior research for the survey.

McCutcheon also used and matched up both Griffith's Valuation and the first edition Ordnance Survey maps and Memoirs of the 1830s. This was an important feature of his county survey of industrial and commercial sites such as corn mills, scutch mills, spinning mills and weaving factories and mines. Having sifted through all this information, McCutcheon plotted the industrial sites on to modern maps which were used for this fieldwork. The valuation material was put on to cards and filed alphabetically by county, parish and townland. Some 2,000 of these are available in the archive. They contain details of the owner, the building's dimensions and the quantity of goods produced. In addition, the archive contains details of business ledgers, taken from PRONI records, yielding information on the history of Ulster businesses. There is also material gleaned from local papers and professional journals.

The photographic archive, within the McCutcheon Archive, has over 20,000 black and white prints and negatives stored in metal cabinets. There are three sections: transport and communications, a county-based coverage of mills, factories and extractive industries, and finally a photographic survey of Belfast. There are over 2,000 additional miscellaneous photographs, of which only 250 are labelled. The fieldwork, conducted between April and October in the years 1962–8, resulted in descriptive notebooks illustrated with sketches, for each area and site surveyed. These are supplemented with other relevant documents such as company brochures, bill-heads and pamphlets. The notebooks also contain the author's percipient comments on all aspects of the fieldwork, such as weather, people and countryside. The value of all this to the local historian is obvious. Further details on the McCutcheon Archive, are in 'The McCutcheon archive: a survey of industrial archaeology', in *Ulster Local Studies*, vol 15, no 1, Summer 1993, by Noreen Cunningham. See also, in the same issue, Nick Brannon, 'The Monuments and Buildings Record, Hill Street, Belfast'. Much of the industrial heritage of Ulster is also covered in the massive volume by McCutcheon, *The Industrial Archaeology of Northern Ireland*, HMSO, Belfast and London, 1980. This is replete with photographs, maps, sketches and commentaries. See also pp 85–92 on photography.

ARCHIVES AND RECORD OFFICES IN THE REPUBLIC OF IRELAND

THE NATIONAL ARCHIVES
Bishop Street, Dublin 8. Tel (01) 478 3711; fax (01) 478 3650
The Reading Room at Bishop Street is open from 10.00am to 5.00pm, Mon–Fri, excluding public holidays. Archives are produced to readers between 10.00am and 12.45pm and between 2.00pm and 4.30pm. A current reader's ticket is a prerequisite for using the Reading Room and can be obtained on the first visit.

The National Archives was established in June 1988 through the amalgamation of the Public Record Office of Ireland (founded 1867) and the State Paper Office (SPO) (founded 1702) formerly at Dublin Castle. The headquarters is at Bishop Street and though there are premises at the Four Courts, they are not open to the public. When archives still held at the Four Courts are requested, they will normally be produced at Bishop Street by 1.00pm on the following day. There is an introductory leaflet, from which most of the following is taken, available at the issue desk.

- Archives stored in the main building at Bishop Street: archives of government departments post-partition; archives formerly held at the Four Courts. The most frequently used archives held at the Four Courts and Public Record Office have been moved to Bishop Street and include the following: Census 1901; Census 1911 (not yet open to the public in the Public Record Office in Northern Ireland); Census 1821–51 (fragments); cholera papers (Board of Health); Famine Relief Commission; National Schools applications, registers and files (pre-1922); Valuation Office and Boundary Survey; archives salved in 1922 (part); Church of Ireland parish registers; Ferguson Manuscripts; genealogical abstracts (Betham, Crossle, Groves, Grove-White and Thrift); Irish Record Commission; Lodge's Manuscripts; O'Brien set of Encumbered Estates Court Rentals; will books and grant books; archives acquired from private sources (M, D, T, 975–999, 1000–series, etc); trade union archives.
- Archives moved from Dublin Castle: Rebellion Papers; State of the Country Papers; Chief Secretary's Office Registered Papers (1790–1922); Official Papers; Outrage Papers; Convict Reference Files; Privy Council Office; Chief Crown Solicitor's Office.

    Most of the General Prisons Board Archives are still boxed. The above records, while mainly to do with Dublin Castle's rule in a law and order and security sense, nevertheless are of interest in many cases to the local historian (see pp 53–4 on reports of the District Commissioners of the RIC).

- Archives available only on microfilm: tithe applotment books (35mm microfilm rolls) Primary or Griffith's Valuation (microfiche).
- Archives stored at the Four Courts include: court records; Chancery Pleadings 16th-18th century; wills, 1900–73; archives salved in 1922 (part); Companies Registration Office; National School salary books; Office of Public Works (part); Ordnance Survey (part); Prison Registers; Quit Rent Office (part), known as Headfort Papers; business records; Boards of Guardians' records; hospital records.
- Archives stored in the Bishop Street warehouse: General Prisons Board (part); Office of Public Works (part); Ordnance Survey (part); Quit Rent Office (part); map collection.
- At Bishop Street, there are many map collections from different sources. These include Down Survey maps, manuscript estate maps, OS collections of material relating to the first edition series such as townland boundary survey maps, surveyors notebooks, fair plans. There are 19th-century hand-drawn 5 inch and 10 inch town plans, Board of Trade maps (annotated from OS maps), OPW maps of canals, railways and navigation.

Reference works
On the public shelves in the Reading Room at Bishop Street there are many reference works such as the Irish Manuscripts Commission publication of the Quit Rent Office records, edited by Robert C Simmington, the Civil Survey 1654–6, vol 3, counties Donegal, Derry and Tyrone, the Pender Census of Ireland 1659, Lewis' Topographical Dictionary, the Primary Valuation and Tithe Applotment index of surnames and the General Topographical index for the 1901 Census, etc.

THE ROYAL IRISH ACADEMY (RIA)
19 Dawson Street, Dublin 2. Tel (01) 676 2570/676 4222; enquiries to librarian.
Opening hours: Mon (except Jul–Sept, closed at 5.30pm); Tue–Fri 9.30am–5.30pm, closed for two weeks in August.

Set up in 1785 as the Irish Academy, the epithet Royal was added the following year. It was very much an Ascendancy creation which reflected the interest in antiquities of the leisured class of the time. The library is primarily for the use of members but serious researchers may be granted access to it after a strict procedure has been followed. There is a major collection of manuscripts in Irish from the early Celtic monastic period to the 20th century, including the *Annals of the Four Masters*. These are listed in the *Catalogue of Irish Manuscripts in the Royal Irish Academy*. The library has a large collection of pamphlets and periodicals based on the *Proceedings of the Royal Irish*

Academy. Other collections include records of the Ordnance Survey, antiquarian notebooks and sketches. The Haliday Collection has over 2,000 volumes of pamphlets 1682–1859 and tracts 1578–1859 which are catalogued on a chronological basis.

(The following has been taken from *Source Material for Local History in the RIA Library*.) The RIA Library has many printed books on county and local history, etc.

Manuscript sources
General
1. Ordnance Survey Manuscripts 1825–41.
(a) Memoirs: 52 boxes for 20 counties
Antrim, 17 boxes; Armagh, one box; Cavan, one box; Donegal, two boxes; Down and Louth, three boxes; Fermanagh, two boxes; Londonderry, 20 boxes; Longford, Mayo, Meath, Monaghan, one box; Tyrone, two boxes.
(b) Letters, extracts and inquisitions: 137 vols – Antrim and Londonderry; Armagh and Monaghan; Breifny; Cavan and Leitrim; Donegal; Down; Fermanagh; Londonderry. Rev M O'Flanagan's typescript of Ordnance Survey letters, except Antrim, Cork, Tyrone. 1834–41, 35 volumes.
(c) Ordnance Survey maps of the counties of Ireland 1832–44, 38 volumes.
(d) Du Noyer and Wakeman: Ordnance Survey Sketches from 13 counties, 11 volumes, 12 T 1–11.
2. Books of Survey and Distribution of Forfeited Lands in Ireland, 17th century, 17 volumes.
3. The Reduction of Ireland. Collection of 17th century original documents, seven volumes, 24 G 1–7.
4. Charters of Irish Towns (copies), 12 volumes, 24 Q 7–18.
5. Book of postings and sales of forfeited lands 1702–03, one volume, 24 Q 34.
Manuscript copy of original printed edition.
Examples of manuscripts relating to particular counties: County Antrim: S McSkimin (1) Historical notes and collections of newspaper cuttings in Co. Antrim 1828. 1 vol 24 Q 2. (2) Recollections of Co. Antrim 1795–99 1 vol. 24 F 36. Proceedings and resolutions at public political meetings in Co. Antrim 1763–99 1 vol. 24 K2. List of landholders etc. counties Down and Antrim nineteenth century. 1 vol. 24 K 19.

LIBRARY OF THE OFFICE OF PUBLIC WORKS
51 St Stephen's Green, Dublin 2. Tel (01) 661 3111; fax (01) 661 0747
Enquiries to librarian, ext 2159. Access to OPW staff, others by appointment, inter-library loan. Photocopying is available. *Opening hours:* Mon–Fri 9.30am–12.30pm, 2.00pm–5.00pm

The Office of Public Works (OPW) was established under 'An Act for the Extension and Promotion of Public Works in Ireland', passed on 15 October 1831. Its first report was in January 1833. The Library of the OPW, at St Stephen's Green, contains the Annual Reports from 1831, which are very detailed and of great use to the local researcher. These include records of most public works in Ireland 1831–, including public buildings, national monuments, fisheries, harbour development, inland navigation, land improvement, arterial drainage, relief schemes, housing and railways. Plans and drawings of the work carried out are included.

The bulk of the archives of OPW are now deposited in the National Archives (see pp 101–2). A 300-page *Guide to the Archives of the Office of Public Works* by Rena Lohan, has recently been published. The OPW archive also holds the Record of the Archaeological Survey and the Sites and Monuments Record of Ireland.

The OPW Library at St Stephen's Green contains the Technical Library, The Monuments Library, Records of the Waterways and the Wildlife Service. There is a computer catalogue of current records held by OPW. There is a book-stock of some 13,500 volumes, 11,000 periodicals, audio-visual stock 290 items and 160 video cassettes. For further information on the Library at St Stephen's Green, see the article by the librarian, Valerie M Ingram in *GLINT*, the Government Libraries Information Newsletter, no 11, January 1996.

THE REGISTRY OF DEEDS
King's Inn, Henrietta Street (off Bolton Street), Dublin 1. Tel (01) 733300
Opening hours: Mon–Fri 10.00am–4.30pm

An Act of Parliament of 1708 set up a central office in Dublin to deal with all transactions concerning the legal side of the ownership of land such as con- veyancing, mortgages and leases. As such, it came at the start of the period of Irish history in which an emerging Protestant landowning aristocracy and gentry, to become known as the Ascendancy, was busily putting down roots in the countryside and through the Penal Laws, extinguishing and replacing the last vestiges of the former Catholic land-owning class. The Registry of Deeds was to be the agency of this process. Indeed the statute setting it up stated that it was

> for securing purchases, preventing forgeries and fraudulent gifts and conveyances of land tenements and hereditaments, which have been frequently practised in this kingdom, especially by Papists to the great prejudice of the Protestant inter- est thereof.

This extract indicates clearly the policy of the Irish parliament in reducing

Catholic land-holding. From 1704, Catholics were forbidden to buy a lease for more than 31 years or take up a mortgage, a situation that was only ended in the 1780s. Land owned by Catholics was by law divided equally among their sons, thus through time dramatically reducing the size of catholic holdings. However, if a son became a Protestant, he got all the land even while his father was still alive. It is estimated that half of the 1,700 Catholic landowning families shifted religious affiliation during the 18th century. The registry also includes 'bills of discovery' which were part of the Penal code against Catholic ownership of land over a certain acreage. A Protestant who discovered this could file such a bill to claim it. Most however, were filed by Protestant friends to save the Catholic landowner from a hostile 'bill of discovery'. The success of all this can be clearly seen in the fall of Catholic land ownership to less than 5 per cent by 1800. In the Penal era restrictions on land ownership were placed on dissenting Protestants as well, a fact which is highlighted by the very few deeds registered from that quarter in this period.

The deeds were registered by copying them either in complete form or in abstract. Known as 'memorials' they were stored in vaults in lead-lined boxes. The transcriptions were copied into huge heavy 'abstract and transcript' books in date order each containing 600 leaves of parchment, with accompanying indexes. There are two indexes, the name index, in alphabetical order, and the land index, arranged in volumes by county. In the land index, each county is subdivided into baronies and each barony into townlands, arranged alphabetically. The earliest name index volumes cover the years 1708 to 1729, while those of the land index are from 1708 to 1738. Both have been subsequently served by a series of indexes covering consecutive periods. These are on microfilm in the National Library in Dublin. PRONI has a microfilm copy of the indexes as well as of the memorial books themselves, ref. MIC/311.

The registration of deeds generally related to transactions between people of roughly the same social stratum, who might conceivably become embroiled in litigation with one another. It hardly ever affected the 'lower social orders', few of whom were lease-holders. Most leases were kept within the landlord's collection of estate papers. The Registry of Deeds, although it probably contains a small proportion of those executed, nonetheless is an important archive which houses some 3 million deeds. It holds, in addition to deeds, leases, business transactions, marriage licences and settlements and wills. It is, perhaps because of its daunting size, still a comparatively untapped resource for historians.

THE FOLKLORE ARCHIVE, THE DEPARTMENT OF IRISH FOLKLORE, UNIVERSITY COLLEGE, DUBLIN (UCD)

The archive is housed part in the Arts Building, UCD main campus, Belfield and part in Earlsfort Terrace (Irish folk music section), central Dublin. The manuscript archive and departmental library at Belfield are accessible to scholars and the general public from 2.30pm–5.30pm, Monday to Friday except for the month of August. Access to sound and pictorial collections and to the Irish folk music section is by special arrangement only.

The Department of Folklore at UCD is the immediate successor of the Irish Folklife Commission (1935–71). In addition to its teaching mission, the department continues the work of the commission in the collecting, classifying, study and exposition of all aspects of Irish folk tradition. The holdings include two manuscript series, the main manuscripts amounting in 1993 to 2,238 bound volumes, and the schools collection of 1,128 bound volumes and 1,124 boxes of unbound material. There are many thousands of hours of sound recordings on disc and tape, around 40,000 photographs, films, video tape as well as plans, sketches, diagrams and other pictorial representations of the visible aspects of tradition. There is also a specialist library of some 38,000 printed books, pamphlets and periodicals. Approximately three-quarters of the manuscript and sound holdings are in Irish, most of the remainder being in English, along with some material in other Celtic languages.

The archive covers all the counties of Ireland. There is a broad range of material relating, not only to all aspects of folk narrative tradition, but also the entire field of material folk culture, as well as folk music song and dance. The 14 main topics are:

- Settlements and dwelling
- Livelihood and household support
- Communications and trade
- The community
- Human life
- Nature
- Folk medicine
- Time
- Principles and rules of popular belief and practice
- Mythological tradition
- Historical tradition
- Religious tradition
- Popular 'oral literature'
- Sports and pastimes.

The main bulk of the material was assembled by full-time collectors, but much was compiled by enthusiastic amateurs. The 'Schools Scheme' of 1937–8, covering the 26 counties, was carried out by school children aged 11–14, who followed specially prepared guidelines. The only Ulster counties involved in this were Cavan, Monaghan and Donegal. The contents of the manuscripts are covered by four card indices as follows: collectors; informants; provenance (giving province, county barony and parish or district); and subject matter. The collection has been increasing steadily over the years. Prospective users of the archive are advised to give advanced notice of their subject of enquiry and date of arrival. Major parts of the collection are available at various third-level institutions and the Schools Collection for a number of counties is available at county libraries.

8

MUSEUMS

The relevant major museums in Northern Ireland are the Ulster Museum, the Ulster Folk and Transport Museum, the Ulster-American Folk Park, Armagh County Museum, Enniskillen Castle Museum and Heritage Centre, Irish Linen Centre and Lisburn Museum. Cavan, Donegal and Monaghan each have a county museum. As well as their displays and exhibitions of objects, these museums are also major holders of records of local interest. The collections in the National Museum of Ireland in Kildare Street, Dublin, are not so much orientated towards local history as such. There has been of late a proliferation of heritage centres in both jurisdictions, some of which are valid sources of information about the locale, though not in the same archival league as the major record holders. The Northern Ireland Tourist Board produces an information bulletin, *Stop and Visit,* an excellent guide to heritage and visitors' centres, many of which are worth a visit. The Office of Public Works publication *Heritage Sites 1995*, however, lists only four Ulster sites, all in Co Donegal.

MUSEUMS IN NORTHERN IRELAND

THE ULSTER MUSEUM
Botanic Gardens, Belfast BT9 5AB. Tel (01232) 381251; fax (01232) 665510 *Opening hours*: Mon–Fri 10am–5pm, Sat 1–5pm, Sun 2–5pm. Botanic Gardens; free. Shop, cafe. Wheelchair access, adapted toilets, parking on request.

Material relevant to the study of local history is held in all three curatorial divisions of the Ulster Museum. The division of science is responsible for artefacts relating to Ulster's industrial heritage, particularly factory linen production, while the division of art is made up of the Department of

Applied Art, which cares for material relating to Irish costume and textiles, ceramics and pottery, toys and childhood, and decorative furnishings; and the Department of Fine Art, whose collections of paintings, watercolours and prints include many items of local interest and relevance.

Responsibility for the collections curated in the division of history is shared between the Department of Archaeology and Antiquities, which holds artefacts informing the history of Ulster from the earliest human settlements; and the Department of History, which is responsible for material relating to the history of Ireland since 1600. The history department's collections include the broad areas of numismatics and banking, horology, the Post Office, locally produced paper ephemera and the history of local printing; Irish civil and military uniformed groups; domestic miscellanea; and the iconographic collections of maps, prints and watercolours, and the photographs of Irish historical and topographical importance (see pp 86–7). The history department also houses a substantial archive collection of primary and secondary sources relating to the local history of Ulster. Of course, the general public of necessity will not have ready access to this treasury of sources, which is mainly for the use of the curatorial staff of the museum. Nevertheless the staff will provide expert advice and help to the serious researcher.

COLLECTIONS

The Welch Manuscripts, around 29 volumes of diaries, notes, memoranda and negative lists of Robert J Welch (1859–1936), leading Belfast photographer and naturalist (see p 86 on his photography). Historical and topographical collection of over 1,000 negatives, old and new. The Local History Department has over 250 maps, 1,500 topographical drawings, paintings and prints, around 250 portraits. For the major RJ Welch and AR Hogg and other photographic collections in the museum, see pp 86–7 on photography in this book.

THE ULSTER FOLK AND TRANSPORT MUSEUM
Cultra, Holywood, Co Down BT18 0EU. Tel (01232) 428428; fax (01232) 428728
Opening hours: the library is open daily during office hours.

The museum is set on a 177-acre site seven miles from Belfast on the road to Bangor. The indoor and outdoor exhibits show how people lived, worked and spent their leisure time. The outdoor exhibits consist of original buildings, from all over Ulster, reconstructed as they would have looked c.1900. This is of interest particularly to historians of vernacular architecture. The

Transport Museum has an award-winning Irish railway collection and many examples of historic modes of transport on land, sea and air. It highlights particularly the contribution made by Ulster inventors like Ferguson and McCandless and the shipbuilding industry of Belfast.

The museum has an excellent library and archive designed to support research by both museum staff and the general public, on a reference basis. It contains about 18,000 books and periodicals, many of which are of local interest. The archives are equally large in scope, containing reminiscences, folklore material, railway timetables maps and much more. The photographic collection reflects the activities of the museum and includes:

- WA Green Collection.
- Rose Shaw Collection.
- Dundee Collection.
- *Belfast Telegraph* Collection (viewing by appointment).

Research material on microfilm
- Census material.
- Census material for Ireland 1821–1911. Printed returns; 11 volumes of fiche.
- Parish of Dunaghy, Co Antrim, 1851. Original MS census returns, two reels.

Maps
First edition Ordnance Survey 6-inch maps of Ireland 1829–1842 (survey dates), 32 volumes fiche.

Folklore
Sixty-nine reels, containing microfilm on various aspects of non-material culture.

Newspapers
- *Belfast Election* 1868; one reel.
- *Belfast Newsletter* 1738–1930; 339 reels.
- *Belfast Protestant Journal* 1846–50 and January 1885–February 1886; three reels.
- *Belfast Weekly Advertiser* 1879–84; four reels.
- *Guardian and Constitutional Advocate* 1832; one reel.
- *Weekly Observer* 1868–72; five reels.
- *Downpatrick Recorder* 1836–1973; 64 reels.
- *Londonderry Journal* 1 June 1773– 2 June 1776; one reel.

Periodicals
Irish Builder 1859–1900; 18 reels.

Topographical
Ordnance Survey Memoirs, 1830s; 22 reels.

Miscellaneous
Reports of the Commissioners of Education in Ireland, 1834–1920, seven volumes; fiche.

The Sound Archive
This is sited in the museum administration building. It was established by Act of Parliament, to reflect the way of life and traditions of the people of Northern Ireland, past and present. It contains some 3,000 tapes to which there is a card index. There are a dozen volumes of selected transcriptions of these. The topics covered range the full gamut of topics germane to local history. There is a substantial published catalogue.

BBC Radio Archive
See p 147.

THE ULSTER-AMERICAN FOLK PARK

Mellon Road, Castletown, Omagh BT78 5QY. Tel (01662) 243292
Opening hours (library): 9.30am–4.30pm

The outdoor section is of use to the local historian in its precise re-creation of vernacular architecture including a Famine cabin, 19th-century forge, weaver's cottage, replica of Mountjoy Presbyterian church, Mellon Homestead, Campbell House, Tullyallen Mass House 1768, Hughes House, Castletown National School, Mountjoy Post Office 1861, 19th-century Ulster street, Blair's Printing Shop, emigrant ship and Dockside Gallery. Traditional crafts such as blacksmithing, coopering, woodturning, strawwork, needlework, patchwork, spinning and bread making are all demonstration crafts at the park.

The research library is primarily a centre for migration studies. It also supports the park's main activities with reference resources on Ulster and the United States in the 18th and 19th centuries and the link between the two. The other main themes are agriculture, architecture, biographies and autobiographies, social customs and religion and traditional crafts. Material held in the library includes books, journals, maps, microforms, and audiovisual material.

The Emigration Database contains information on all aspects of Irish emigration to North America from the early 1700s to the 1900s. It consists of ships' passenger lists, emigrant letters, family papers and diaries, shipping

Pathways to Ulster's Past

advertisements, newspaper reports, deaths and marriages of former emigrants, births of children to Irish parents, government reports and statistics of Irish emigration to America and illustrated material showing ship types, ports, routes and maps, shipboard conditions and the cost of the voyage to America. The database may be accessed in the library at the park and also at the local history departments of the Library Area Boards in Armagh, Ballymena, Ballynahinch, Belfast, Derry and Omagh. It is as well to make an appointment and an administration fee may be charged.

ARMAGH COUNTY MUSEUM
The Mall East, Armagh City BT61 9BE. Tel (01861) 523070; fax (01861) 522631
Opening hours: Mon–Fri 10am to 5pm; Sat 10.00am to 1.00pm and 2.00pm to 5.00pm, Sundays closed.

The museum is housed in a fine Georgian building, built in 1834 as a school house. It became the headquarters of the Armagh Natural History and Philosophical Society and was acquired by the local council in 1931. As well as being the county museum, with one of the finest county collections in Ireland, it is also the regional branch of the Ulster Museum. It has a fine reference library which, while strongest on Co Armagh, also has information on other parts of the country.

The museum library was largely built up by Thomas GF Patterson, curator 1935–63. It largely reflects his major interests of historical and genealogical research, especially relating to Co Armagh. He and friends and colleagues established a huge collection of printed and manuscript material much of it rare and valuable in all senses of the word. The Patterson collection includes bound typescripts of hearth money rolls, depositions and voters' lists of the 17th and 18th centuries, copied before the destruction of the Four Courts. Patterson also collected pedigrees, leases and grants and the Griffith manuscript valuation books of 1839. The collection contains a great number of printed books of local and genealogical interest. There are some 25 typed volumes, written by Patterson, known as *Ardmachiana* or sometimes *Armagh Miscellany*, covering a wide range of topics. This is indexed.

Other collections include the Armagh Militia Records 1793–; the Charlemont estate papers for the 19th century and estate leases 1750–1829. There are copies of records relating to Co Armagh: Poll Book 1753; Hearth Money Rolls, 1664; Muster Roll, 1630; Census of Armagh City, 1770; Armagh Presbyterian Church Registers, 1727–9, 1796–1809; Manor of Armagh Tenants, 1714. The papers of the prominent and historic Portadown family of Blacker are of great importance to the library's collection. The collection of AG Sloan of Ballyworkan House contains important sources of local and genealogical interest. The collection of HG Tempest of Dundalk is also important in the field of local history.

The County Library acquired, from the library of the Armagh Natural History and Philosophical Society, a facsimile copy of the Book of Armagh, no 313 of the limited edition edited by Professor J Gwynn and published by the Royal Irish Academy in 1913, while the museum got eight volumes, including O'Curry's Lectures on the manuscript materials of ancient Irish history (Dublin, 1861). The library subscribes to many periodicals and has acquired many reference books. The library has a map and print collection of interest to the local historian. The article by former curator Roger Weatherup 'Armagh County Museum – the Reference Library', in *Irish Booklore*, vol 2, gives a very comprehensive account of the museum's holdings of documents.

DOWN COUNTY MUSEUM AND ST PATRICK'S HERITAGE CENTRE

The Mall, Downpatrick BT30 6AH. Tel (01396) 615218; fax (01396) 61550
Opening hours: June-Aug: Tue-Fri 11.00am-5.00pm; Sat 2.00pm-5.00pm; Sun 2.00pm-5.00pm; Mon 11.00am-5.00pm; Sept-May closed Sun, Mon; open St Patrick's Day, Easter Monday and May holidays.
Admission free, disabled access. Limited shop, tea-room, free parking facilities.

The museum and heritage centre occupy the restored buildings of the late 18th-century Down County Gaol. As well as being a county museum, Down is very much concerned with the Patrician heritage of the surrounding area, and has on display many early Christian and medieval specimens from ecclesiastical sites.

The museum also houses an extensive book collection amounting to c.6,500 volumes. The photo archive has Lawrence and Welch prints. The County Down Photographic Collection has a topographical index. It includes the work of Thomas Gribben of Loughinisland who was a farmer and photographer who recorded the political and cultural events in Loughinisland, Co Down, from the Home Rule Crisis 1912 to World War Two. Also there is the work of Dan J McNeill, a photographer who recorded life, in and around Dundrum, Co Down, from the 1940s to the 1960s.

HARBOUR MUSEUM DERRY CITY

Harbour Square, Derry BT48 6AF. Tel (01504) 377331; fax (01504) 377633
Opening hours: Mon–Fri 9.00am–1.00pm and 2.00pm–5.00pm by appointment only
Enquiries to the archivist.

The archives provide a comprehensive record of the growth and development of the city from the late 17th century and include:
- Council minute books (1673–86; 1688–1704; 1720–36; 1742–1969).
- Rural District Council minute books (1908–69).
- Standing and Sub-Committee minute books (1918–69).
- Letter books and correspondence files (1849–1980).
- Charts, maps and architectural plans (1877–1973).
- Legal documents (1679–1970).
- The archives also contain a limited amount of private material such as local business, trade union and literary records.

FERMANAGH COUNTY MUSEUM
Enniskillen Castle, Castle Barracks, Enniskillen, Co Fermanagh BT74 7HL. Tel (01365) 325050 or 325000 ext 244; fax (01365) 327342

Built as the medieval home of the Maguires, Enniskillen Castle now houses the Heritage Centre, the Castle Keep, Watergate and the Arcaded Barracks. The Castle Keep houses the Museum of the Royal Inniskilling Fusiliers and displays about the castle. The Arcaded Barracks houses displays about Fermanagh's archaeological and historical monuments. The Heritage Centre

Hackett's Drapery Shop, High Street, Enniskillen, Co Fermanagh c.1905 (possibly as late as 1910). The proprietors Joseph and his sister Bridget Hackett stand between two members of staff. The sign in Irish reads MacEocaid teac na n-earraide ndeas *– Hackett, house of nice merchandise. (Fermanagh County Museum)*

has award winning audio-visual and visual displays about Fermanagh and there are county related archives. The collections contain newspapers, books, maps, manuscripts, records, sound archive and photographs. They are particularly related to Co Fermanagh. The collections can only be viewed by appointment. Fermanagh County Museum provides research files on many aspects of Fermanagh, eg social history, early history, geography, archaeology, etc.

Main holdings:
- Local government.
- Co Fermanagh criminal book, 1861–1969.
- Land-holding and sales posters.
- County assize proclamations.
- Parish of Derrymacausey Primary School Register 1844–54.
- Ephemera dealing with entertainment, sport, politics, religion and organisations in Co Fermanagh.

THE IRISH LINEN CENTRE AND LISBURN MUSEUM
Market Square, Lisburn, Co Antrim BT28 1AG. Tel (01846) 663377; fax (01846) 672624
Opening hours (library): Mon–Fri 9.00am–5.00pm

The Irish Linen Centre is an excellent permanent exhibition on the history of the Irish linen industry. This in itself is of interest to many local historians and well worth a visit. Adjoining it is the Lisburn Museum itself, which contains material on the Lisburn and the Lagan Valley area.

Newspapers
Lisburn Standard and *Lisburn Herald*, a partial coverage of years 1898–1964. There are approximately 30 periodicals in stock.

Maps and plans
These include Ordnance Survey and others covering Lisburn and the Lagan Valley.

Other documentary material
There is a small archive collection.

Photographs
There is a range of photographs and slides covering Lisburn and the Lagan Valley and the historical and modern processes of the linen industry.

Other media
Video and audio tapes; microfilms, including the 1901 census enumeration schedules of Lisburn and the Lagan Valley district.

Subject coverage
Irish history, especially Ulster and the history of Lisburn and the Lagan Valley; linen technology; costume and fabrics.

Special collections
The library of the former Lambeg Industrial Research Association (LIRA), comprising some 2,000 books, journals, manuscripts, technical reports and photographs of all aspects of the linen industry.

Catalogue
Reference library: card catalogue, author and subject. LIRA library, awaiting re-cataloguing. Computerisation under review.

Clientele
Staff members and, by appointment, members of the general public.

Services
Reference and lending for staff, reference only for researchers, students and the general public. Enquiries answered.

Facilities
Photocopying, microfilm and microfiche reader/printer facilities. Photographic orders can be undertaken, subject to copyright clearance.

Publications
The Huguenots and Ulster 1685–1985, an illustrated catalogue, *Flax to Fabric: the Story of Irish Linen*, published as an illustrated souvenir of the permanent exhibition in the Irish Linen Centre.
    All enquiries should be addressed to: Research and Publications Officer.

MUSEUMS IN THE REPUBLIC OF IRELAND

THE NATIONAL MUSEUM OF IRELAND
Kildare Street, Dublin 2. Tel (01) 677 7444; Fax (01) 676 6116
Opening hours: Tue–Sat 10.00am–5.00pm, Sun 2.00pm–5.00pm. Closed: Mondays, Christmas Day, Good Friday.

The collections of the National Museum of Ireland cover archaeology, history, the decorative arts, folk life, geology and zoology. The museum holds an extensive photographic archive, including a number of collections such as the Mason Collection (rural life, mainly from the 1920s and 1930s), the St Joseph Collection of Aerial Photographs (archaeology and landscape) and the Cashman Collection (political and current affairs, emphasis on 1916–23). Archives of the Natural History Museum include notebooks and journals of naturalists whose collections are held by the museum, 1850–.

The Archaeological Collection has artefacts from every county in Ireland. Early Christian monasteries, etc are well documented. Research on these is possible through the Museums Registers and Topographic Files. The latter contain illustrations, description of objects, excavation plans, correspondence with finders, etc. There is a waiting list for research facilities, particularly during the summer months, and researchers should contact the Keeper of Irish Antiquities in advance.

The Historical Collection covers the principal events in Irish history from 1770–1923 and includes documents, memorabilia, uniforms, arms, etc. The Folklife Collection has a comprehensive archive of photographs and objects, relating to the domestic and working life of people from the 18th to the 20th centuries. The Decorative Arts Collection covers the same period and encompasses costume, textiles, glass and ceramics. Access to files and registers can be arranged through the relevant keeper. Information on any aspect of the museum's collections can be obtained from the Education Service.

CAVAN COUNTY MUSEUM

Virginia Road, Ballyjamesduff, Co Cavan. Tel (049) 44070; fax (049) 44332
Opening hours: 10.00am–5.00pm weekdays, weekends by appointment.

The museum, housed in the former St Clare's Convent and situated off the main Ballyjamesduff–Virginia Road, opened to the general public in January 1997. It is 'committed to the collection, documentation, conservation and display of the material culture of County Cavan and surrounding districts.' As such it is complementary to the mainly archival aspect of the County Library. A number of private collections have contributed to the new museum. For instance, Mrs P Faris of Cornafean has given part of her own 'pighouse collection' to the museum. Other significant artefacts are on loan from other museums around Ireland.

DONEGAL COUNTY MUSEUM

High Road, Letterkenny, Co Donegal. Tel (074) 24613
Opening hours: Tue–Fri 11.00am–4.30pm, Sat 1.00pm–4.30pm
Closed: lunch-time 12.30pm–1.00pm

A replica of the three-faced Corleck head, an Iron Age celtic pre-Christian artefact, dated between 2nd century BC and 2nd century AD. The original is in the National Museum, Dublin. (Cavan County Museum)

The museum is housed in a fine old stone building which was once part of the Letterkenny workhouse. It has exhibitions of objects relating to the recent history and folk life of the county. Copies of the Donegal Railway and the Londonderry and Lough Swilly Railway Company records are stored in the County Museum but are not at present available to the public.

MONAGHAN COUNTY MUSEUM AND ART GALLERY
1–2 Hill Street, Monaghan. Tel (047) 82928
Opening hours: Tue–Sat 11.00am–1.00pm, 2.00pm–5.00pm

The museum was established in 1974, by the county council, the first local authority museum in the state. There is a large local history section. It houses early maps, a good example of which is Richard Bartlett's 1603 map of Monaghan, a Grand Jury plate (1839–40) of Mason's Ironstone, uniforms of Monaghan militia of the late 19th to early 20th century, tools of local industries and crafts and many fine examples of the famous Carrickmacross lace. The main document collections of use to the local historian are:

- Various Monaghan estate papers, 18th to 20th century.
- Marron Collection of extracts from records relating to Co Monaghan in the PRO, London, National Archives, Dublin, and the Marquis of Bath's Archive at Longleat House, Wiltshire.
- Monaghan County Council minutes, rate books, ledgers 1899–1959.
- Miscellaneous records, including Monaghan Urban District Council, Clones Petty Sessions, Monaghan County Infirmary, Castleblaney Workhouse 19th to 20th century.
- Collections of papers of Charles Gavan Duffy (1816–1903) and Senator Thomas Toal (1911–42).

9

LIBRARIES

In Northern Ireland, there are five education and library boards and the library headquarters of each are repositories of many records of Irish and local interest. There are also branch libraries with records relating to particular locales. Local studies librarians play an invaluable role in assisting the education sector, the public, and local studies groups in their areas, due to their expert local knowledge and the wealth of material at their disposal. There are in addition celebrated ancient libraries such as the Linen Hall Library in Belfast and the Armagh Public Library. In the Republic of Ireland, each of the three Ulster counties has its own county library. The National Library of Ireland in Dublin complements the National Archives in its major holdings of archives, records and books of interest to the local historian.

LIBRARIES IN NORTHERN IRELAND

THE BELFAST CENTRAL LIBRARY, HUMANITIES AND LOCAL STUDIES DEPARTMENT

Royal Avenue, Belfast BT1 1EA. Tel (01232) 243233; fax (01232) 332819
Opening hours: Mon and Thur 9.30am–8.00pm; Tue, Wed and Fri 9.30am–5.30pm; Sat 9.30am–1.00pm
Opening hours (newspaper library): Mon and Thur 9.30–7.30pm; Tue, Wed and Fri 9.30am– 4.30pm; Sat 9.30am–1.00pm

The Humanities and Local Studies Department has the largest collection of Irish material held by a public library in Northern Ireland. It has more than 50,000 books, maps and pamphlets, extensive holdings of newspapers, periodicals, government publications and other special collections. The last guide to the local and Irish studies collections was published in 1979 and so is undoubtedly out of date. Therefore, the normal route of access to its collections must be, of necessity, through the catalogues and information guides, situated facing the information counter. The local studies collection is primarily for reference use only. Photocopying and microfilm facilities are available.

The library has a comprehensive collection of Irish bibliographies. It has a large selection of early Belfast printed books. As well as the well-known statistical surveys of Dubourdieu, on Antrim and Down, published respectively in 1802 and 1812, there are 18 others for different counties carried out between 1800 and 1830. There is a strong section on local industry, with much pamphlet and emphemeral material. The John Horner collection of 200 volumes is a great source on the linen industry. There is a large holding of facsimiles of the great works in the Irish language. The biography and genealogy section contains much of interest to the local historian. For instance, the 17th-century Montgomery Manuscripts provide an excellent source for the plantation in Co Down. There is a fine collection of travellers' tours of Ireland, for example Arthur Young's *Tour in Ireland* (1780) or J Gamble's *View of Society and Manners in the North of Ireland* (1813). The library has a large number of books on all aspects of Belfast history, including Pilson, Benn and Owen. There are many major works on Irish antiquities.

Periodicals and directories
The library has a large collection of periodicals dealing with local studies, including long and complete runs of all major Irish periodicals. There is also a comprehensive collection of directories, almanacs and annuals.

Government publications and papers
Government publications, including the papers of the Irish Parliament prior to 1800, and the 19th-century British Parliamentary Papers on Ireland, are available, as are Griffiths and the other valuation records. There is also an extensive collection of local government minutes for Northern Ireland, poll-books and electoral registers, including the earlier poll books, lists of how electors voted.

Patent library
This is a comprehensive source for patents taken out for inventions by Ulster people.

Maps
There are over 10,000 maps, with fine Irish specimens, dating back to the 16th century, including examples by Baleu, Mercator, Ortelius, Petty and

Speed, with a particularly fine series of hand coloured maps in 28 original leather cases. There are general and specialised maps relating to Belfast as well as large-scale maps of other towns. The library holds many of the Ordnance Survey maps to various scales.

Archives and manuscripts
This is an extensive collection which includes the correspondence and personal papers of several of the major benefactors of the library. The most notable of these is the FJ Bigger (1863–1926) Collection comprising some 40,000 items, reflecting his involvement in the history and politics of Ulster. The Bryson and MacAdam Collection comprises 44 volumes of manuscripts, dating from the late 18th and early 19th centuries, dealing with the Irish language in Ulster. It may only be consulted on microfilm. The AS Moore (1870–1961) Collection contains 1,000 items, comprising cuttings, pamphlets, indexes and local history compilations, with a special emphasis on local industry. AS Riddell (1874–1958) has left a collection of some 5,000 items, comprised of cuttings, indexes and compilations on social history and local biography.

Photographs
Major photographic collections include the work of F Frith, RJ Welch, AR Hogg, and WA McCutcheon. The Lawrence Collection, from the National Library in Dublin, is available on microfilm. There are more recent photographic surveys including the aerial photography of Aerofilm Ltd, from 1950.

The newspaper library
This is one of the largest collections of newspapers in Ireland. It is an excellent resource for local history. As well as the major British and Irish national dailies, the collection houses provincial papers from Ireland north and south, including titles found nowhere else in Ireland. It has virtually complete runs of the *Belfast Telegraph, Newsletter, Irish News* and *Northern Whig*, as well as the Belfast radical paper *The Northern Star* (1792–7). The formats are either bound volumes or microfilm. Readers are free to photograph or transcribe from bound volumes. There is a small charge for exposure of microfilm copying. Photocopying from bound volumes is at the same rate. As the newspaper facility is in the basement, prospective readers should apply at the reception desk in the humanities and local history reading room. A member of staff will provide an escort to the newspaper library. The library has a series of fully indexed cuttings books covering local newspapers from the turn of the century. This is possibly the single most used resource in the library and it provides also an introduction to the local newspapers themselves.

North Eastern Education and Library Board (NEELB)
There are two main Irish and local studies collections in the NEELB area.
These are held in the Area Reference Library and the Irish Room.

THE AREA REFERENCE LIBRARY, BALLYMENA
Demesne Avenue, Ballymena BT43 7BG. Tel (01266) 41531 ext 31; fax
(01266) 46680
Opening hours: Mon–Thur 10.00am–8.00pm; Tue–Wed 10.00am–5.30pm;
Fri 10.00am–6.00pm; Sat 10.00am–5.00pm

THE IRISH ROOM, COLERAINE
Divisional Headquarters, County Hall, Castlerock Road, Coleraine BT51
3HP. Tel (01265) 51026

Both the Area Reference Library, Ballymena and the Irish Room are reference libraries only. Arrangements can be made to consult reference copies at
local branches. The material held includes books, government publications,
newspapers, magazines, maps, photographs, postcards, records, tapes, slides,
films and microfilms. As well, all branches have local and Irish material and
there are local history packs, specific to the branch areas, duplicates of which
are held in the Area Reference Library. The Library Service publications
include reading lists on different places, people and events. *Local Collection*
is a quarterly publication of books of local and Irish interest, available in all
branches. There is a Support for Publications scheme which encourages the
publication of material on the north-east area, by giving financial assistance
towards printing and publication costs. Further details from the Chief
Librarian, Area Library HQ, Demesne Avenue, Ballymena BT43 7BG. The
Local Studies Librarian is at present busily contacting all local history
groups in the area for information on their work, which will be collated
centrally.

Newspapers
The Area Reference Library, Ballymena holds most local newspapers in the
North Eastern Area from their first issue. Others are held in branch libraries
and can be traced in the NEELB *Newspaper Holdings* printed catalogue.
- *Ballymena Advertiser* 1873–92.
- *Ballymena Guardian* 1970–.
- *Ballymena Weekly Telegraph* 1894–1966, known as *Ballymena Times* during
  1966–70. In 1970 it was incorporated with the *Ballymena Observer* 1857 to
  date.
- *Larne Times* 1891–1962, then known as *East Antrim Times* 1962–May 1983.
  From May 1983 three editions of the *East Antrim Times*.

- *Larne Times* 1983–.
- *Carrickfergus Times* 1983–.
- *Newtownabbey Times* 1983–.

The Carrickfergus Library holds the *Carrickfergus Advertiser* 1884 to date. The Larne Library holds some duplicate copies of the original *Larne Times*. The Irish Room, Coleraine holds the following:

- *Ballymoney Free Press* 1870–1934.
- *Coleraine Chronicle* 1844–.
- *Coleraine Constitution* 1877–1908, since then known as *Northern Constitution* to present day.
- *Derry Journal* 1971–80.
- *Derry Standard* 1937.
- *Londonderry Sentinel* 1851–7, 1929–53, 1971–80.
- *North Antrim Standard* 1890–1922.
- *Northern Herald* 1860–63.

It is not possible to take photocopies from bound newspapers. If a paper is on microfilm, it can be photocopied from the reader/printer in the Area Reference Library, Ballymena. Readers should ring in advance to book this very popular facility.

Journals
There is a wide range of journals covering local and Irish history. In Ballymena there local history society journals like *The Corran, The Glynns, Carrickfergus and District Historical Society Journal*, as well as province-wide journals such as *Ulster Folklife*.

Photographs
Both reference libraries have collections of photographs and postcards relating to the North Eastern area. Most are from the Lawrence Collection, copies of which can be got from the National Library in Dublin. As well, a collection of photographs is being assembled from local donors.

Maps and town plans
These cover the North East area as follows, indicating where located in the Area Reference Library (Ballymena) or the Irish Room (Coleraine):
- Ordnance Survey County Series Antrim (in Ballymena and Coleraine Libraries) and Londonderry, 1830s, 1850s, scale 6 inch to 1 mile (only in Coleraine). Coleraine has Ordnance Survey County Series maps for Londonderry 1904, scale 6 inch to 1 mile and 1930, scale 25 inch to 1 mile. It also has Antrim for the 1930s, scale 1 inch to 1 mile (sheets 1–9) and Northern Ireland 3rd Series 1960s, scale 1 inch to 1 mile (sheets 1–9).

- Maps to accompany Griffith's Valuation counties Antrim and Londonderry 1862, scale 6 inch to 1 mile (in both libraries).
- Town plans for towns and villages in the North East area 1830s–1905, various scales (in both libraries).
- Geological Survey of Ireland 1870s, scale 1 inch to 1 mile (in Coleraine).
- Northern Ireland Geological Survey 1952, scale ¼ inch to 1 mile (in Coleraine) and 1966, scale 1 inch to 1 mile (in Coleraine). Both libraries have Admiralty Charts.

The Irish Room in Coleraine has Co Derry townland maps and a collection of other historical maps. Maps can be sent to local branches for consultation only.

Southern Education and Library Board (SELB)

THE IRISH STUDIES LIBRARY, LIBRARY HEADQUARTERS

1 Markethill Road, Armagh BT60 1NR. Tel (01861) 525353; fax (01861) 526879
Opening hours: Mon and Wed 9.30am–7.15pm; Tues, Thurs and Fri 9.30am–5.00pm

This library has a wide-ranging stock covering all aspects of Irish life and learning from the earliest times to the present day. The sections, of interest to local historians, are categorised below.

Architectural guides and area plans
Surveys outlining architectural features of buildings in towns, villages and surrounding rural areas throughout most of Northern Ireland. Detailed analyses of specific areas and proposals for their future development.

Arts and leisure
As well as general works on the arts, crafts and sports, there is a considerable collection of individual club histories.

Autobiographies and biographies
Of local and unknown people as well as the famous.

Church history
As befits the ecclesiastical capital, there is a large holding of books, pamphlets and journals, some rare and valuable, pertaining to individual parishes and to the wider church.

Geography and travel
In this section is an enviable collection of the impressions of visitors, known and unknown, past and present, to these shores.

History
Studies of Irish history from a wide range of approaches and emphases make up a considerable proportion of the library's stock. There are many works which are out of print and difficult to obtain elsewhere.

Local studies
Library staff compile information packs on the history, culture, economic activities and other significant features of most of the towns, villages and parishes throughout the area covered by the SELB. These are particularly useful for school or other in-depth studies of specific areas.

Maps
Large-scale representations of most of the area covered by the SELB from the 19th century to the most recent ordnance survey. Detailed street maps of many major towns and villages are also available.

Newspapers
The library contains at least one newspaper from each locality within the SELB area. Some of these go back to the 18th and 19th centuries and many are on microfilm.

Parliamentary Papers
The library's sizeable collection includes material on education, poverty, land, transport and law and order.

Photographs and postcards
The library has copies of the Lawrence Collection. Towns and major villages within the SELB area can be seen as they were in the 1970s in photographs taken by the Department of the Environment. The postcard holdings include scenic views of the past.

Politics
This section includes rare pamphlets dating from the 17th century as well as more recent journals and papers.

South Eastern Education and Library Board (SEELB)

THE IRISH AND LOCAL STUDIES COLLECTION
Library Headquarters, Windmill Hill, Ballynahinch, Co Down BT24 8DH.
Tel (01238) 562639, exts 235/236/237; fax (01238) 565072
Opening hours: Mon–Fri 9.00am–5.15pm. Telephone queries and visitors are welcome. If possible telephone in advance to make an appointment.

The collection comprises over 30,000 volumes on Ireland and Irish life. Special emphasis is laid on Ulster and particularly on Co Down and South Antrim. The Irish material in branch libraries is only a small part of the collection, the bulk of which is held at Library Headquarters in Ballynahinch. As well as books, there are 'Pender's' Census of 1659, Dubourdieu's Surveys of Antrim and Down, 1802 and 1812 respectively, and most 19th and 20th century directories and almanacs. The Library has Griffith's and other valuation records, OS and town maps, OS parish memoirs, newspapers and access to the Emigration Database at the Ulster-American Folk Park.

Maps
Over 3,000 sheets are stocked, some dating from the early 19th century. There are Ordnance Survey Parish Memoirs for the parishes in the Board area.

Photographs and postcards
These include over 1,000 postcards, mostly Victorian and Edwardian, and photographs relating to Down, South Antrim and Belfast. The Lawrence Collection is on microfilm and there are indexes to the Welch Collection.

Periodicals
A range of important periodicals is held.

Newspapers
There are indexed files of local newspapers since 1970. On microfilm there are *Belfast Telegraph* 1939–45 and from 1976; *The Newsletter* 1738–1925, the *Irish Times* from 1859 to date. Reader printers are available at Bangor, Downpatrick, Dairy Farm (Twinbrook/Poleglass) and Headquarters.
The following are the most important newspaper holdings:
- *County Down Spectator* 1904–64.
- *Downpatrick Recorder* 1836–86.
- *Mourne Observer* 1949–80.
- *Newtownards Chronicle* 1873–1900.

- *Newtownards Independent* 1871–3.
- *Newtownards Chronicle* 1901–39.
- *Northern Herald*: an index to Co Down and Lisburn items, 1833–6.
- *Northern Star*: an index to Co Down and Lisburn items, 1792–97.

The library also compiles comprehensive folders of cuttings and other information on topics of local interest: agrarian crime and civil disorder in Co Down 1837–86; The Ards, brick and lime works; quarries and mining in County Down; Castlereagh, Clandeboye, Comber, Donaghadee; homicides, infanticides and suicides in Co Down 1836–86; Irish Freemasonry; Killyleagh and Crossgar, the Mournes; Norman Ball (Bangor inventor); Strangford Lough.

As well, the library has published a very useful booklet *Local History Projects: What the Teacher Needs to Know*. There is a very large selection of local history packs available on loan to schools. A great deal of genealogical material is listed in the pamphlet *Family History, The Bare Bones*, including on microfiche, the International Genealogical Index of the Mormon Church, containing 88 million names. Full details of publications can be obtained from the headquarters and branch libraries.

The Western Education and Library Board (WELB)
Like the other Library Boards, the WELB is connected by terminal to the Ulster-American Folk Park Emigration Database. There are three divisions in the Board: Tyrone, based in Omagh; Derry, based in Derry City; and Fermanagh, based in Enniskillen.

OMAGH LIBRARY
1 Spillars Place, Omagh BT78 1HL. Tel (01662) 244821; fax (01662) 245118
Opening hours: Mon, Wed, Fri 9.30am–5.30pm, Tue and Thur 9.30am–8.00pm, Sat 9.30am–1.00pm, 2.00pm–5.00pm

There is an extensive Irish and local studies department to which a guide, *Local History Sources* was produced in 1982. Much of the following comes from it and other leaflets compiled by former local studies librarian Kate McAllister. On the shelves, there is a section of books on Tyrone (catalogue number 941.64).

As well as the usual topographical dictionaries, directories and topographical writings (travellers' descriptions of Ireland), there are:
- *The County Tyrone Directory and Almanac* for 1896, 1902, 1904 and 1905.
- *Directory for Belfast and the Province of Ulster*, 1880.
- *The Dungannon and District Almanac and Diary* for 1902.

- *The Omagh Almanac and County Tyrone Directory* for 1882, 1883, 1885,1886, 1889, 1890, 1891, 1892, 1893, 1896, 1898.

There are also local histories and guide books under 941.64. The library also has a number of church and parish histories for specific localities.

Official statistics and surveys
These include published volumes of *Agricultural Statistics of Ireland* (previously *Returns of Agricultural Produce in Ireland*) for most years between 1849 and 1898, which give information by county, barony, Poor Law Union or electoral division on the types and qualities of crops, stock and land. In some volumes numbers of scutch mills are given. There are typed extracts from Board of Guardian Minute Books for Castlederg and Strabane around the Famine years. Other items of local interest include Parliamentary Papers (Blue Books); census figures, the population of each town and townland in Co. Tyrone is available for the following years:1841, 1851, 1861, 1871, 1881, 1891, 1901, 1911, 1926, 1937, 1951, 1961, 1971. In addition population figures for towns, parishes and baronies can be seen on microfiche for 1821 and 1831.

Earlier surveys and lists include: Hearth Money Rolls 1666, a typed copy of the list covering Co Tyrone; Irish Militia List 1761 (again a typed copy for Co Tyrone); Muster Rolls 1631; Simington, Robert *The Civil Survey AD 1654–1656, Counties of Donegal, Londonderry and Tyrone, Vol 3*, with the returns of church lands for the three counties; John McEvoy, *Statistical Survey of County Tyrone*, Dublin Society 1802; Ordnance Survey Memoirs, typed extracts for Tyrone parishes of Aghaloo, Aghalurcher, Ardstraw, Artrea, Cappagh, Clogherney, Donacavey, Donaghedy, Dromore, Drumglass, Drumragh, Kilskeery, and Termonamongan (see pp 46–9); Municipal Corporation Boundaries 1837. For Tyrone there are letters, reports and plans, and maps for Dungannon and Strabane.

Journals and periodicals
The library holds many of interest to the local historian.

Newspapers
There are many newspapers, both national and local, held in Omagh in bound copies or on microfilm. I have included here only those for Tyrone pre-partition. A full list can be obtained from the library or in the *Northern Ireland Newspaper Holdings*.
- *Dungannon News* 1893–1900.
- *Mid-Ulster Mail* (Cookstown) 1891–1916, 1918–19, 1922–83.
- *Omagh News* 1862–1869, 1871–2.

- *Strabane Chronicle* 1899, 1912–22.
- *Strabane Morning Post* 1823–37.
- *Strabane Weekly News* 1912–22.
- *Tyrone Constitution* (Omagh) 1844–89, 1891–.
- *Tyrone Courier* (Dungannon) 1880–87.
- *Tyrone Herald* (Strabane) 1892–1900.
- *Tyrone Tribune* (Omagh) 1898–9.
- *Ulster Herald* (Omagh) 1902–.

Maps and plans
The bulk of the library's maps are copies and therefore not of perfect quality. Co Tyrone and Co Fermanagh Ordnance Survey county series 6 inch to 1 mile, 1830s, 1850s, 1900s. The Co Tyrone 1900s edition is imperfect.
- Towns and villages in Co Tyrone.
- Town plans, various scales, 1834–.

Photographs and postcards
The library has a collection of well over 1,000 photographs, both new and copies of old shots, collected mainly for local history exhibitions. They are indexed by the subjects that appear in them. The Lawrence Collection is held on microfilm. A small collection of postcards from Co Tyrone is held.

Ephemera
Folders about towns and villages in Tyrone are kept in the local history department in Omagh. They consist of copies of pages from books, articles from journals and newspapers, etc which cover various aspects of the life in each place. Copies of the files about Omagh, Newtownstewart, Baronscourt, Ardstraw, Castlederg, Sion Mills, Strabane and Fintona are held in the nearest public library. There are additional files being compiled on subjects like hiring fairs, Belleek, emigration, house types, and so on. As they come into the department all books are checked for any mention of local places and an index to these references is kept.

FERMANAGH DIVISIONAL LIBRARY
Halls Lane, Enniskillen BT74 7DR. Tel (01365) 322886; fax (01365) 324685
Opening hours: Mon, Wed, Fri 9.15am–5.15pm; Tue and Thur 9.15am–7.30pm; Sat 9.15am–1.00pm.

The former librarian FJ Nawn drew up a collection of some 22,000 books of Irish interest. He was also responsible, with Kate McAllister, for a 1982 pamphlet *Local History Sources, Fermanagh Division*. Although there have been additions to this since, it nevertheless still provides a good guide. Much of the following has been taken from it. The library holds the usual topographical dictionaries, almanacs and directories and of more local interest, *Lowe's Fermanagh Directory and Household Almanac for 1880* and *The Handbook or Directory for the County of Fermanagh*, Charles Macloskie, 1848. There are local histories, journals and guide books, too numerous to list. There are also many church and parish histories, family histories and histories of buildings.

Official statistics and surveys
These include:
- Board of Guardian Minute Books. Typed extracts are available for around the Famine years for Enniskillen and Irvinestown.
- British Parliamentary Papers 'Blue Books'.
- Census figures for each town and townland in Fermanagh for the following years: 1841, 1851, 1861, 1871, 1881, 1891, 1901, 1911, 1926, 1937, 1951, 1961, 1971.
- Griffith's Valuation for this part of Ireland was carried out in 1862. The following unions or part-unions are contained in Co Fermanagh— Ballyshannon, Clones, Enniskillen, Irvinestown and Lisnaskea. Information in these volumes includes the names of all tenants in each townland and town with a description of their land and property including acreages and annual rateable valuation.
- There are copies for Fermanagh of Hearth Money Rolls 1665; Muster Rolls; Irish Militia List 1761.
- John O'Donovan's letters containing information relative to the antiquitities of Fermanagh collected during the progress of the Ordnance Survey, 1834–5.

Local newspapers on microfilm
- *Enniskillen Advertiser* 1864–76.
- *Enniskillen Chronicle and Erne Packet* August 1808–February 1811, 1824–May 1849, from Aug 1849 continued as *Fermanagh Mail and Enniskillen Chronicle*.
- *The Enniskillener* February 1830– December 1836, January 1840–February 1840.
- *Enniskillen Watchman* September–October 1848.
- *Fermanagh Mail and Enniskillen Chronicle* August 1849–November 1850, March 1851–December 1859, 1861–2, 1864–93.
- *Fermanagh News* 1896–1900.
- *Fermanagh Sentinel* March 1854–January 1855.
- *Fermanagh Times* March 1880–1900.
- *Impartial Reporter* 1839–73, 1879–84, 1886, 1888–96, 1899–1950, 1987–June 1995.

Maps and plans
The library has some 1,443 printed maps. The holdings include:
• Co Fermanagh and Tyrone Ordnance Survey county series 1830s, 1850s, 1900s, scale 6 inches to 1 mile (Co Tyrone 1900s is imperfect).
• OS Irish Grid Co Fermanagh 1:10,000, Co Fermanagh 1:2,500, Co Fermanagh 1:1,250.
• Pre-OS maps, Fermanagh barony maps, originals in PRONI. A few county and Ulster maps 1685.
• Towns and villages in Co Fermanagh 1834 to the present. Town plans, various scales.

Photographs
Prints from the Lawrence Collection, are mainly of Enniskillen and Belleek although copies can only be obtained from the National Library in Dublin.

Ephemera
Files about towns and villages in Co Fermanagh have been made from photocopies of maps, from history books, articles from journals, census figures, etc. Each file is kept in the nearest library or trailer library to the town or village concerned. A copy of each is kept in the library in Enniskillen.

DERRY CENTRAL LIBRARY
35 Foyle Street, Derry BT48 6AL. Tel (01504) 2272300, ext 279; fax (01504) 269084
Opening hours: Mon and Thur 9.15am–8.00pm; Tue, Wed, Fri 9.15am–5.30pm and Sat 9.15am–5.00pm

The library houses the Irish Collection with useful material for local historians studying Derry. There are many books of local interest, eg *Eglinton, a Thriving Ornament*, B. Mitchell. There are the usual periodicals on various Irish subjects.

Photographs
A growing collection of historic photographs of Derry, includes the Lawrence Collection and some photographs from the Bigger and McDonald Collection, Willie Carson and James Glass (of Gweedore in west Donegal).

Newspapers
• *Derry Journal* 1838–1993.
• *Londonderry Sentinel* 1829–1993.
• *Londonderry Standard* 1830–1900, bound volumes 1955, 1956, 1957, 1958, 1961 and 1962.

- *Londonderry Guardian* 1857–71.
- *Belfast Telelegraph* (north-west pages only) 1887–8, are on microfilm.

Newspaper files
These have been collected to cover all aspects of Derry life from local factories to Derry City Football Club. Local and national papers are indexed daily.

Historic buildings files
A city of great historical importance, Derry has many outstanding and interesting buildings. There are for example, files on St Columb's Cathedral, the Lunatic Asylum and the Grianan of Aileach, nearby in Co Donegal.

Maps
These include a number of siege and plantation maps, maps of the city and county in the 1850s, 1870s and early 1900s, as well as the modern Ordnance Survey maps.

The Famine
The library has published a catalogue, commemorating the 150th anniversary of the Great Famine giving a list of the many sources available, in the Irish Collection, on it and subsequent emigration. This includes a great number of books, fact and fiction, periodical articles, newspapers, photographs (of post-Famine Donegal by James Glass) and relevant sketches from the *London Illustrated News*.

OTHER LIBRARIES

ARMAGH PUBLIC LIBRARY
Abbey Street, Armagh BT61 7DZ. Tel (01861) 523142; fax (01861) 524177
Opening hours: Mon–Fri 10.00am–1.00pm and 2.00pm–4.00pm, and at other times by appointment.
Guide: *Catalogue of Manuscripts in the Public Library of Armagh*

Known generally as the Robinson Library, after its founder in 1771, the Church of Ireland Archbishop of Armagh, this is very much a church-orientated archive. Built to the design of Thomas Cooley, the inscription over the public entrance in Greek means 'the medicine of the mind'. Archbishop Robinson's personal library contains 17th and 18th-century books. It includes in its holdings rare manuscripts and books, including St Catherine of Siena's dictated trance visions and *Gulliver's Travels*, annotated by Dean Swift, who is associated with Armagh. Important collections include those of William Reeves, Bishop of Down (1882–96) relating to Irish church history from the 5th to the 19th century; the correspondence of Lord George Beresford, Archbishop of Armagh (1822–62); records of 17th and 18th-century primatial visitations; copies of Armagh primatial registers.

THE LINEN HALL LIBRARY
17 Donegall Square North, Belfast BT15GD. Tel (01232) 321707
Opening hours: Mon–Fri 9.30am–5.30pm; Thur 9.30am–8.30pm (5.30pm closing in July and August); Sat 9.30am–4.00pm

Membership is by annual or life subscription. The Linen Hall acts as a public reference library for members and non-members alike. This is Northern Ireland's leading private library. Founded in 1788, it takes its name from the White Linen Hall, in which it was housed, from 1802 until January 1892, when it moved across the street to its present home, a former linen warehouse. This was due to the White Linen Hall's demolition to make way for the present City Hall. The library grew out of the radical and intellectual ferment of late 18th century Belfast. The United Irishman, Thomas Russell, 'the man from God knows where', was an early librarian. Henry Joy McCracken was a committee member. The library has been a fixture in the cultural and intellectual life of Belfast for more than two centuries. It has a very large Irish collection, with many holdings unique to the Linen Hall. There is the world renowned collection of political pamphlets and ephemera. The present Deputy Librarian, John Killen, has written the excellent *A History of The Linen Hall Library 1788–1988*. I have gleaned much of this information on the library from this.

The major collections are as follows:

Archives
The Belfast Printed Books Collection is a microcosm of Belfast history and culture over 300 years. An extensive and very important genealogical and heraldic collection is kept on the second floor. This includes directories, tombstone inscriptions, church registers, published family histories, printed pedigrees, heraldic visitations, wills, marriage licences, hearth money rolls, emigrant lists, indexes to births, deaths and marriages in local papers.The Blackwood and Greeves manuscripts, presented by former presidents of the Belfast Library and Society for Promoting Knowledge, the full official title of the institution, are an important part of this. These have been indexed as a dictionary catalogue since 1986.

Theatre archive
The theatre collection, of some 3,000 items, is a record of the north's

An actor called Burnham, from JF Warden's Old Theatre Royal Stock Company, as Claude Melnotte in The Lady of Lyons. The photograph was taken by D Welch in 1871. (Linen Hall Library Theatre Archive)

theatrical experience in the 20th century, reflecting the work of playwrights, actors and managers and portraying the precarious existence of Ulster theatre companies. There are manuscript meteorological records for Belfast, 1796–1906. The Joy manuscripts, consist of selected materials for the annals of the province of Ulster, collected by Henry Joy in the late 18th and early 19th centuries. The library holds the minutes of the Belfast Literary Society, 1801–.

Maps

The map collection, begun in the 18th century has many rare, unique and ancient maps. The library sells prints of some of these. As well, there are the 6 inch Ordnance Survey maps of Ireland, county and town maps and manuscript maps of some estates and demesnes.

Newspapers

The library holds a very large collection of newspapers: *Belfast Newsletter* 1738–, the longest-running daily newspaper in the British Isles; *The Northern Star* 1792–7 the paper of the United Irishmen; *Belfast Commercial Chronicle* 1805–55; the *Northern Whig* 1824–1963. As well as coverage of 20th-century papers, there is a unique holding of northern papers of limited life-span, which only exist in the Linen Hall. These include the *Belfast Citizen* 1886, *Belfast Evening Citizen* 1875, *International News* 1889, *Irish Sport* 1904, *Labour Advocate* 1885, *Newry Journal* 1776, *Downpatrick Star* 1955, *Telegraph Bulletin* 1920, *Tyrone Free Press* 1894, *Tyrone Independent* 1872 and *Ulster Star* 1896. In 1979 the checklist of *Northern Ireland Newspapers* was compiled by the then librarian, JRR Adams. There is also a fine collection of periodicals, dating from 1739, covering a wide range of interests.

Postcards

Another unique feature is the extremely large collection of photographic postcards and views. This is an immense source for the local historian. There are some 5,000 cards, the bulk held in 'Royal Mail Postcard Albums'. There are interesting political cards dealing with the 1907 Belfast Docks Strike, the anti-Home Rule agitation 1912–14 and the Easter Rising of 1916. Sadly, these are as yet largely uncatalogued and the researcher must plough through the relevant shelf area.

Books

The library holds a large number of collections of books, manuscripts, maps, prints, etc, donated by individuals which bear the names of the benefactors. These cover a wide range of topics, especially of Irish and local interest.

Prominent in these are the collections of RR Belshaw, RS Lepper, Lavens M Ewart, SAG Caldwell and William McCready.

The Sentry Hill Collection, the as yet uncatalogued papers of the Co Antrim McKinney family, contain items of local interest particularly in relation to Ulster-Scots heritage, including the 'Weaver' poetry of East Antrim. Recently the library has become a popular venue for lecture series, and even drama productions, many of which deal with Irish and local history.

LIBRARIES IN THE REPUBLIC OF IRELAND

THE NATIONAL LIBRARY OF IRELAND
Kildare Street, Dublin 2. Tel (01) 661 8811; fax (01) 676 6690
Opening hours: Mon 10.00am–9.00pm; Tue–Wed 2.00pm–9.00pm; Thur–Fri 10.00am–5.00pm; Sat 10.00am–1.00pm
Manuscripts reading room and readers' ticket applications (valid tickets are required): Mon 10.00am–12.30pm, 2.00pm–5.00pm, 6.00pm–8.30pm; Tue–Wed 2.00pm–5.00pm, 6.00pm–8.30pm; Thur–Fri 10.00am–12.30pm, 2.00pm–4.30pm; Saturday 10.00am–12.30pm

The National Library was founded in 1877 as a result of the Dublin Science and Art Museum Act. The Royal Dublin Society Library and the Joly Library constituted its foundation collections. The Library and the complementary National Museum is housed in classical style in buildings designed by the Cork-born architect Sir Thomas Deane. There are two main guides to the library, of interest to the local historian, from which most of the following has been gleaned: *Local Studies Sources in the National Library of Ireland and Using the National Library*.

Published guides to sources
Manuscript Sources for the History of Irish Civilisation, Boston, 11 volumes, with an index, 1965, by R Hayes, former Director of the National Library of Ireland. William Nolan, *Tracing the Past: Sources for Local Studies in the Republic of Ireland*.

Printed books and pamphlets
Consult the subject volumes of the printed books catalogue under the name of your village and town and parish and county. This will ensure that you will find any books or pamphlets which deal even in part with your locality. Items acquired since 1968 are listed in a separate card catalogue. There is a comprehensive selection of directories, almanacks and town directories. Those relating to individual towns or counties will be located through the printed

books subject catalogue. General directories are on open access (ask staff for directions).

Periodicals and articles in magazines

To trace any articles relating to your locality which have been published in Irish magazines anytime prior to 1970, consult *Periodical Sources for the History of Irish Civilisation*, a nine-volume published catalogue (edited by RJ Hayes 1970), which indexes all articles, reviews, obituaries and any other substantial items which appeared in a range of Irish periodicals or magazines prior to 1970. Entries are arranged by person, subject place and date. The places volume has entries are arranged by county with places within counties in alphahetical order. As well as looking for entries relating specifically to your area you should also check those relating to your county. Pamphlets (items of less than 100 pages) are not yet included in the printed books catalogue. A handwritten catalogue of the some 19,000 pamphlets is available on microfilm.

Newspapers

To find newspapers, which were published in your locality, consult the alphabetical newspaper list. It has a list of provincial papers arranged by place of publication and details of the National Library's file for each title. The collection goes back to 1690. Also *Newsplan* (1992) gives holdings in the National Library, the British Library and other locations.

Maps

Printed and manuscript maps are listed in the map catalogue. Entries are arranged alphabetically by place: check all the entries relating to your county as well as those relating to your specific locality. The first edition (1833–46) of 6-inch Ordnance Survey maps for your locality might be studied in conjunction with revised editions (first revised editions date for particular counties from 1855 to 1893). A revised edition on a larger scale (1:2,500) was begun after 1887. Also there are large-scale plans of towns., mainly 'five-foot', published in the second half of the 19th century. In conjunction with the first Ordnance Survey two sets of descriptive papers covering the whole country were compiled mainly under the direction of John O'Donovan. These are the OS Name Books and OS Letters and consist of topographical and antiquarian data on townlands, towns and parishes. There are typescript copies available (No. Ir. 92912 03 (Name Books); Ir. 9141 O2–24 (Letters) there are also copies on microfilm.

Illustrations of places

Consult the one-volume published *Catalogue of Irish Topographical Prints and Original Drawings* (Rosalind M Elmes, revised edition by M Hewson, 1975), which lists over 3,000 illustrations. Entries are mainly by county with indexes of places, masters and engravers at the end of the volume.

For portraits there is the *Catalogue of engraved Irish portraits mainly in the Joly Collection and of original drawings*, also by Rosalind M Elmes.

Photographs of places
There are several collections of photographic negatives which have material on most towns in the country and copies can be provided.
- The Lawrence Collection consists of 40,000 negatives from the period 1870–1914. The main Lawrence Collection catalogue is arranged by alphabetical order of town and county, in a main series catalogue and a new series catalogue. The main series catalogue may be viewed on microfilm. Part of the collection (termed new series) has a catalogue with entries arranged only by county.

Seventeenth-century engraving of Arthur Chichester, 1st Earl of Donegall (1601–74). (National Library of Ireland)

- The Eason Collection consists of 4,090 negatives dating mainly from the period 1900–40; the catalogue is arranged by county.
- The Valentine Collection consists of 3,000 negatives mainly from the period 1900–60. The catalogue is arranged on cards by county and town. In the case of Lawrence new series, Eason and Valentine, there are no microfilm copies so people ordering copies have to rely on the catalogues as the glass negatives are too fragile for viewing by members of the public. Prints may be purchased.

Stereoscopic negatives
A collection of 3,050 negatives of Irish scenes (c.1860–83) which provided twin images for viewing in astereoscope. For example there are 18 views of Rostrevor, Co Down (SP 1262). The catalogue is indexed by county and town.

Manuscripts
For local material consult the Places volumes of the published catalogue *Manuscript Sources for the History of Irish Civilisation* (edited in 11 volumes by RJ Hayes, 1965). This includes manuscript material material of Irish interest in repositories and in private custody in Ireland and overseas. Entries are arranged by county with places within county in alphabetical order: it is wise to check all entries for your county as well as for your particular place. Also check Places section of the supplement, covering material catalogued in the period 1965–75. In addition, a card catalogue of material processed in the library since 1975 is available in the Manuscripts Reading Room.

Architectural drawings
A list on card of some 5,000 architectural drawings, mainly of the 18th and 19th centuries, held in the National Library and of the National Library's architectural drawings in the Irish Architectural Archive. Those in the National Library may be consulted by appointment with the prints and drawings librarian.

British government publications
The library has the full set of over 7,000 volumes of British Parliamentary Papers, often termed 'Blue Books'.

Irish government publications
Generally, these do not have such comprehensive data as 19th-century British government publications and their use for the purposes of local studies is limited. However certain series are obviously important, for instance census data published periodically from 1926 and the *Statistical*

Abstract of Ireland published annually from 1931. Consult Stationery Office lists and A Maltby and B McKenna, *Irish Official Publications: A Guide to Republic of Ireland Papers with a Breviate of Reports 1922–72*. These catalogues are available at the reading room counter.

THE GENEALOGICAL OFFICE
2 Kildare Street, Dublin 2. Tel (01) 661 8811
Opening hours: Mon–Fri 10.00am–12.45pm, 2.00pm–4.30pm

The Genealogical Office, housed separately in a red brick Venetian-style building at the Nassau Street end of Kildare Street, is nevertheless a part of the National Library. It incorporates the Office of Chief Herald and is the state authority for heraldry, genealogy and family history. The Genealogical Office has produced a research pack which, while primarily for those in search of their family history or for genealogical information in general, nevertheless provides very useful information for the local historian. The pack outlines the principal research sources with information sheets on civil records, parish records, census records, land/property records, wills and the registry of deeds. It also contains a checklist of sources, county source list (you state the county required), parish maps (as requested), notes on 19th-century administrative divisions, research worksheets and a list of local research centres. This is very good value as a starting point for the novice in local history. Of use to the local historian is the records of Sir William Beetham, mainly his abstracts from Irish prerogative wills (30 volumes) and pedigrees (23 volumes).

CAVAN COUNTY LIBRARY
Farnham Street, Cavan, Co Cavan. Tel (049) 31799; fax (049) 31384.
Opening hours (reference room): Mon, Wed, Thur 11.00am–1.00pm, 2.00pm–5.00pm, 6.00pm–8.00pm; Tue and Fri 11.00am–1.00pm, 2.00pm–5.00pm.

The library has published a *Guide To the Local Studies Department*, from which much of the following was taken. It also recommends *Books and Authors of County Cavan* (1965) and *Sources for Cavan Local History* (1978), both by Sara Cullen, as bibliographical and research tools.

The Library Guide includes the following:
• Agriculture.
• *Coote's Statistical Survey of Co. Cavan*,1802 gives a picture of farming in the early 19th century.

Antiquities and archaeology
- An Foras Forbatha: *Index to Heritage Items in Co. Cavan* and *Monuments of Archaeological Interest in Co. Cavan.*
- An Foras Forbatha: *Buildings of Architectural Interest in County Cavan.*

Maps
- 1835 Ordnance Survey maps.
- Farnham Estate maps.
- Down Survey parish maps 1654–9.
- Ballinamore/Ballyconnell drainage and Navigation maps, passing from Lough Erne to the Shannon,1846.

Newspapers
These include:
- *The Anglo-Celt* 1846 to date (dormant 1858–64) on microfilm.
- *The Meath People* 1857–63 on microfilm, edited by Cavan man James O'Reilly, it compensates for *The Anglo-Celt*'s dormant years.
- *Cavan Weekly News* 1864–1907; bound original issues, some missing.
- The writings of Bridie M Smith, which appeared in *The Anglo-Celt* are in an album, as are the articles of Dr Philip O'Connell from various papers.

There is a file of different articles from local and national papers on Cavan. Also on file are *The Anglo-Celt* articles about Cavan place-names by 'An Scolaire Bocht', Robert Vincent Walker, dated 1920–28.

Photographs and topographic prints, c.1800 to the present
Lawrence Collection; Eason Collection; Valentine Collection; portraits of Cavan notables; scenic views; street scenes; Farnham photographic album; prints and drawings of the National Museum of Ireland.

Topography
As well as the usual directories, etc, there are many other such sources, one very important of which is the index of materials for the history and topography of Cavan in the Ordnance Survey Records.

General archive material
- There is a collection of church and parish histories.
- Folklore and genealogical material relating to the county.
- Collection of legal documents, leases, rentals, wills, for Co Cavan 18th and 19th centuries.
- Diary of Randal McCollum, Presbyterian Minister, Shercock, Co Cavan, describing social conditions, 1861–71.

- Registers, account and fee books, inspectors' reports from Bailieboro Model School, 1860s–1900s.
- Rural District Council Minute Books, 1899–1925.
- 1584 Fiants, legal records listing the principal people living in the various districts.
- 1664 Hearth Money Rolls, including edited articles for various Cavan parishes.
- 1761 Poll Book for the county of Cavan, on photocopy, listing 1,137 free-holders participating in the election of knights to a parliament in Dublin.
- 1766 Religious Census instituted by the Irish House of Lords.
- 1821 Census. Although most of this was destroyed in the Four Courts fire of 1922, copies had been made by the County Grand Jury and survive for various Cavan parishes.
- 1823–7 Tithe Applotment Books.
- 1825 Registry of Freeholders, compiled and printed in Cavan town.
- 1856–7 Griffith's Valuation.
- 1880 Tenants in the Barony of Clankee giving name, quality of land and yearly rent, the tenure of each tenant, the right of way and other easements.
- Microfilm material relating to Co Cavan.
- 1641 Depositions of Rev George Creighton and Rev Henry Jones.
- 1641–1703 Books of Survey and Distribution.
- 1654–1659 Down Survey parish maps.
- 1600–1800 Irish topographical prints and drawings.
- 1813–58 Reports of the Commissioners of the Board of Education.
- 1821 Census of Ireland, household returns for Cavan parishes.
- 1824–6 clippings from national and provincial papers (including the *Cavan Herald*) on the second or 'new' Reformation in Cavan, with lists of those who conformed to the established church.
- 1824–60 Surname index to Griffith's Valuation and Tithe Applotment Books.
- 1833–4 John O'Donovan's 'Name Books' for Co Cavan place-names. Read also in conjunction with his typescript letters on Cavan.
- 1836 Ordnance Survey extracts for Breifne: extracts from the *Annals of the Four Masters*, from the Pedigree of Don Antonio, Count O'Reilly and from Colgan's *Acta Sanctorum*, with notes by John O'Donovan, collected during the progress of the Ordnance Survey.
- 1841 Census of Ireland: all that remains for Co Cavan is the Parish of Killeshandra. This film is of the individual forms for each household.
- 1846–7 Relief Commission Papers on the attempt to co-ordinate local relief during the Famine.
- 1846 *Anglo-Celt*.
- 1857–63 *Meath People*.

- Various Deputy Keeper's Reports, PROI, relating to Co Cavan.
- 1878 *Landowners of Ireland*.
- 1901 *Townland Index* issued with the 1901 census.
- 1901 census, 24 reels.

DONEGAL COUNTY LIBRARY AND THE COUNTY ARCHIVE CENTRE
County Courthouse, Lifford, Co Donegal. Tel (074) 21968
In order to access the archives in Lifford Courthouse, an appointment must be made with the county librarian who will accompany the researcher throughout.
Open by appointment with the librarian. Photocopying facility.

The Archive Centre, housed in Lifford Courthouse, contains the following collections: Board of Guardian minute books for the period 1840–1925, representing the unions of Ballyshannon, Glenties, Dunfanaghy, Inishowen, Letterkenny, Milford and Stranorlar. They constitute around 800 volumes. The Donegal Town Workhouse records begin in 1914. There are also medical and financial records mainly for Ballyshannon Union and a few admission registers for Glenties, Inishowen and Letterkenny workhouses. Rural District Council minute books exist for some of the unions together with outdoor relief registers and indoor relief registers.

There are many non-catalogued archives awaiting processing. These archives have been inspected and all will be properly catalogued under the requirements on all County Councils of the Local Government Act 1994.
- Grand Jury Presentments 1753–1898 (not complete).
- Register of Freeholders 1768.
- Daniel O'Doherty Collection.
- Dr Maureen Wall Collection.
- Prior Endowed School, Lifford, various records from 1879.
- Co Donegal motor car registers 1903–23.
- Account book, estate of Miss Humfrey 1822–65.
- Griffith's Soil Survey 1834–40.
- Fanad Health Club correspondence 1931.
- Minutes of Donegal Board of Health and Public Assistance 1924–42.
- Minute Book Rural District School Attendance Ballyshannon 1918–25.
- Letters from the Department of Agriculture and Technical Instruction to Co Donegal Committee of Agriculture.
- Book of newspaper clippings 1884–1949.
- Book of newspaper clippings including 18th and 19th century correspondence.
- Volume of photostats of Robert Clements estate 1779.

LETTERKENNY CENTRAL LIBRARY AND ARTS CENTRE
Reference Library, Oliver Plunkett Road, Letterkenny, Co Donegal.
Tel (074) 24950
Opening hours: Mon, Wed, Fri 10.30am–5.30pm; Tue and Thur 10.30am–
8.00pm; Sat 10.30 am–1.00pm

Newspapers
- *Ballyshannon Herald* 1839–70s.
- *Donegal Democrat* 1919–.
- *Derry Journal* 1820s–1984.
- Census Returns 1901 (microfilm).
- Griffith's Valuation (microfilm).
- Congested Districts Board Baseline Reports for Co Donegal 1891 (see pp 63–5 on CDB) (microfilm).
- There are parish records for the following Donegal Church of Ireland parishes from the 1800s: Killaghtee, Killybegs, Inver, Mount Charles.

MONAGHAN COUNTY LIBRARY
The Diamond, Clones, Co Monaghan. Tel (047) 51143; fax (047) 51863
Opening hours: Mon–Fri 9.15am–5.15pm. By appointment with the librarian, research may be allowed on Monday between 6.00pm and 8.00pm

The following is a list of archives and sources.
- Census of Ireland for 1659, Seamus Pender.
- Premiums for sowing flax seed in Co Monaghan in 1796.
- General Valuation of the Rateable Property in Ireland: Union of Monaghan (Griffith 1860).
- Monaghan Grand Jury Presentment Books for 1798, 1811–2, 1824, 1859, 1863–4, and 1869.
- Census of population statistics.
- *Statistical Survey of the County of Monaghan*, CJ Coote (Royal Dublin Society, 1801).
- Ordnance Survey Letters Relating to County Monaghan, John O'Donovan.
- Rentbook Anketell Estate 1784–8.
- Rentbook Newbliss Estate 1840–53.
- Survey of the Estate of Lord Weymouth 1736.
- Survey of the Bath Estate 1851.
- Church Lands of Magheracloone and Magheross 1829.
- Ballybay Estate 1786.
- Book of Inquisition for Monaghan.
- Sites and Monuments Record of Co Monaghan (Office of Public Works).
- Archaeological Inventory for Co Monaghan (Office of Public Works).

Engraving from Co Monaghan in Ireland, its scenery and character etc, *vol III Mr and Mrs SC Hall, London, 1845.*

- The Famine Emigrants 1846–51.
- Irish passenger lists 1847–71 (with passengers place of origin).
- Records of Clones Urban District Council (various) 1899–1977.
- Valuation lists of Carrickmacross, Castleblayney and Clones Rural Districts, with revised lists from 1902 up to 1941.
- Poor Law Records relating to Carrickmacross and Castleblayney Poor Law Unions are in Ballybay Branch Library. Records for Monaghan and Clones Poor Law Unions, whereabouts unknown.

Directories, almanacs and guides
- *County Monaghan Directory*, series 1908–1913.
- *Gillespie's County Monaghan Directory and Almanack*, 1897.
- *Monaghan County Alphabetical List* 1900.
- *Ulster Counties Directory* 1895.

Photographs
These are as yet uncatalogued.

Maps
- Old Ordnance Survey Map, *Monaghan 1907*, Godfrey Edition.
- Ordnance Survey Map of Monaghan 1835–8.

Material on microfilm
- Irish Folklore Commission, National Schools' Collection.
- 1901 Census of Population, Household Returns.
- Grand Jury Presentments for Co Monaghan, 1822–34.
- State of the Country for Co Monaghan 1813–28.
- Outrage Papers for Co Monaghan 1835–52.
- Tithe Applotment Books for Co Monaghan.

Newspapers on microfilm
- *Clones Weekly Chronicle* 1883.
- *Farney Leader* 1908–9.
- *Northern Standard* 1839–1994.
- *People's Advocate* 1876–1906.
- *Monaghan Argus* 1875–81.
- *Monaghan People* 1906–9.
- *The Anglo-Celt* 1846–72 and 1885–1950.

On microfiche
Index of Surnames in Griffith's Valuation and Tithe Applotment Books.

MISCELLANEOUS RESOURCES

Local historians may find the following useful.

BBC RADIO ARCHIVE
The Ulster Folk and Transport Museum operates the BBC Northern Ireland Radio Archive. With the Northern Ireland Library Boards it has a free library loan service whereby radio archive material is made more accessible to students, educationalists, researchers and the public. A copy of the *BBC Radio Catalogue* is available in each library containing information about 1,500 programmes stretching back over the last 70 years. These can be ordered up and listened to in the library. The programmes reflect all aspects of life and culture in Northern Ireland.

THE NORTHERN IRELAND PLACE-NAME PROJECT
The Queen's University of Belfast. Tel (01232) 245133

In 1987, under the directorship of Gerard Stockman, Professor of Celtic, Queen's was commissioned by the Department of the Environment for Northern Ireland to do research into, 'the origin of all the names of settlements and physical features appearing on the 1:50,000 scale map; to indicate their meaning and to note any historical or other relevant information'. The brief was extended to include work on all townlands in Northern Ireland and to bring the work to publication. This has resulted in the *Place-Names of Northern Ireland* series, based on original historical research, of which the following volumes have already appeared:

Vol 1 County Down I Newry and South-West Down, Gregory Toner and Micheál Ó Mainnín

Vol 2 County Down II The Ards, AJ Hughes and RJ Hannan

Vol 3 County Down III The Mournes, Micheál Ó Mainnín

Vol 4 County Antrim I, The Baronies of Toome, Pat McKay

Vol 5 County. Derry I The Moyola Valley, Gregory Toner

Vol 6 County Down IV North-West Down/Iveagh, Kay Muhr

Vol 7 County Antrim II Ballycastle and North-East Antrim, Fiachra MacGabhann.

Information on names not yet published is held on a database. Funding is being sought to continue the research, in the meantime enquiries may be addressed via the Ulster Place-Name Society, c/o Celtic, School of Modern Languages, the Queen's University of Belfast, tel (01232) 273689; e-mail: towns@clio.arts.qub.ac.uk.

Similar research for the southern counties is being carried out at the Place-Names Branch, Ordnance Survey of Ireland, Phoenix Park, Dublin. They have published *Gasaitéar na hEireann*, giving Irish forms of major names and *Liostaí Logainmneachta Muineachán/Monaghan* (Dublin, 1996) has Irish language forms for all townlands in the county.

Local history societies and the Federation for Ulster Local Studies
Finally, among the best resources for anyone involved in the study of local history are the local history societies. Societies, in the nine-county province of Ulster are affiliated to the the umbrella body, Federation for Ulster Local Studies (FULS), 18 May Street BT1 4NL, tel (01232) 235254. Many local societies have knowledgeable skilled practitioners. They organise lectures, outings and conferences and publish journals such as the *Clogher Record*.

FULS, with its executive, development officer and secretary, is an additional resource, and it publishes an excellent journal, *Ulster Local Studies*. There are two indexes for this journal, available from the federation.

FURTHER READING

The following should provide a useful adjunct to the present work:

FHA Aalen, Kevin Whelan, Matthew Stout (eds) *Atlas of the Irish Rural Landscape* (Cork, 1997).

Raymond Gillespie and Myrtle Hill (eds) *Doing Irish local History: Pursuit and Practice* (Belfast, 1998).

Tony Canavan (ed) *Every Stoney Acre has a Name: a celebration of the townland in Ulster* (Federation for Ulster Local Studies, 1991).

W Nolan and A Simms (eds) Sources for Studying the Irish Town (Dublin, 1998).

WH Crawford (ed) *Townlands in Ulster: local history studies*, (Belfast, 1998).

INDEX